HOLES
IN THE
TAR PAPER

HOLES
IN THE
TAR PAPER

A memoir of hits, misses, and ceilings
that leak raindrops and hope

Dan Calloway
with Melanie Calloway

MPG Publishers
M. Patrice Group LLC
Wesley Chapel, NC 28173
www.mpgpublishers.com

Holes in the Tar Paper

Cover Design: Genese Clark

ISBN: 978-0-9965190-8-3 Paperback
        978-0-9965190-9-0 eBook

Other titles by MPG Publishers

Dear Self: A Year in the Life of Welfare Mother
The Mourners' Bench, Aron Seaborn
Stewards of Excellence, Roderick Steward
Suddenly, I Found It! Genese Clark
Maintaining Steady, Tamela C. Stitt

To Sylvia Mae

Contents

GROWING UP

Also Known As

This is not a family tree. We have provided this key as a guide to names used frequently and interchangeably throughout the book. Many southern families went by nicknames growing up. Some names stayed with the individual their entire life.

Daniel and Lucy Calloway
Parents of
Robert Lee Calloway Sr. aka Rob, Robbo, Old-timer

Will and Hanna Jones
Parents of
Sylvia Mae Jones aka Sib, Sylvia Mae, Mama

Robert Sr. and Sylvia Calloway
Parents of
Robert Lee Jr. aka Junior, Gene
Willie Ellis aka Honeyman
Bernard aka Buck
Daniel Wallace Calloway
Aka
Mr. Calloway, Danny, Danny Boy, Dan, Little Brother, Little Man, Shamrock, Sham, The Rock, The All-Star, Daddy, Uncle Danny, Granddaddy, Old Man, The Legend

Anita Faye aka Faye, Little Sister

Fortune in the Land

ACREHOME BOULEVARD WAS AN unpaved road in the middle of somebody's nowhere. The woods. The boonies. This low-lying terrain later became S Avenue, an enclave of small bungalows, ranch, and conch-style homes for working-class families.

Dotted along the rural landscape grew an abundance of cabbage palm, coconut, flame tree, and ash. Wood ticks and chiggers hid in the brush; tree frogs barked from the oaks. Crappie spawned in the shallows of the Earman, a narrow canal that meandered past dense piney woods and sawgrass marshes. Snakes slithered menacingly in the grass.

After World War I, speculators bought plats of this no-man's wasteland, sparking a building boom that lasted through the late 1920s. One such investor was a man named George Currie who, in three phases developed a "colored settlement" called Acrehome Park, its strips of land targeted to rich poor folk brave enough to live among gators, cottonmouths, and mosquitoes fat as stinkbugs.

As far as the eye could see to the north was scrub and sand; water and forest to the west. No Interstate 95. Neighborhood access was via two roads: Acrehome Boulevard and Central Avenue, now known as 28th Street. Dixie Highway, the county main road, ran north and south to wherever we couldn't go. The Florida East Coast railway tracks separated them from us.

The remote inland plats were away from the burgeoning wealth of Singer Island, yet close enough to Monroe Heights to attract brown-skinned laborers with imagination and money. Twenty-five dollars a plot: pittance for the American Dream.

Robert Burns must've been in the area when he wrote "the best laid plans of mice and men often go awry" because in 1928 one of the worse hurricanes to ever hit land swept through the area and destroyed homes, businesses, and claimed thousands of lives. If that wasn't enough to discourage the downtrodden, the Great Depression began one year later. Developers paused or scrapped projects. Investors disappeared North. Bankrupt cities reclaimed property from desperate homeowners for unpaid taxes. Someplace became just another name for hope.

Along comes an indefatigable eighteen-year-old who saw opportunity in the spoils. At once Daddy vowed to own the land. Undeterred by thorn or thistle, he surveyed the area with conviction. A new homestead lay around the bend.

Nestled deep in thicket waist high were barely standing clapboard houses. Slash pine loomed above gently pitched roofs. Overgrown lots brimmed with mango, calamondin, and guava trees; manna rained down from heaven. Rusted water pumps trickled blood and sweat of early settlers. Outhouses hid discretely beneath twining white jasmine. It smelled of warm earth and joy.

To Daddy it was a tropical paradise, a wilderness flowing with milk and orange-blossom honey. For him, buying one lot seemed wise. Purchasing two might stretch his wallet but he saw it as a sensible investment. Mama, having ideas of her own, begged him to buy more. She saw fortune in the land. More acres meant upward mobility and a better life for her family; an opportunity to ensure prosperity and security for generations yet born.

Frugal to a fault, daddy looked at mama and said, "Sib, we gonna buy what we can afford; no more, no less." A day late and a penny short Mr. and Mrs. Robert Calloway Sr. moved into a four-room shack at 3009 Acrehome Boulevard without a care in the world. Two months later, Robert Jr. was born.

Here lived newly married teenagers who had the audacity to believe that with honest work and faith they too could share in the same liberties as whites south of the Mason-Dixon line. Mama and Daddy ventured into the unknown with nothing but willpower, determined to create a loving home for their children.

But for the grace of God my siblings and I were spared a life of scarcity. Our needs were always met; wants never ignored. Daddy was not a risk taker, but he was fearless. Courage proved herself our birthright. Indeed, heroism wells through my veins like the sinuous waves of the Atlantic Ocean: strong, constant.

Years had passed before Daddy shared with me why he didn't get more lots.

"Danny boy," he said. "You remember the first house?"
"Yes sir."

"Son," he said, serious as a man running from his wife, "learn this lesson well. Keep your woman happy but don't give away the store. Never tell her what you earn or what you save. Keep ten percent for yourself. If you earn a hundred, give her ninety. If you save forty, spend four on something worth having; but always keep money for a rainy day."

I don't think Daddy was aware that I knew Mama had kept the family finances from the time they married at Mount Olive, then a one room church with nothing more than a piano and a pulpit. Mama didn't squander money or time. She conserved her husband and household with dignity and grace. But this you can take to the bank: Mama suffered no fool gladly, especially Robert Calloway Sr.

"Danny," she said. "You remember the first house?"

"Yes mama."

"You remember ever wanting for something you didn't get?"

"No mama. I don't."

"Well, no matter what the old-timer tells you, he handed me every bit the whole hundred dollars. I gave him back a ten and spent ten on something worth having."

"Mama, what do you mean?"

"You remember baseball books and mitts and bats?"

"Yes mama."

"Then that's what I mean."

Holes in the Tarpaper

MAMA BIT DOWN ON a piece of leather while daddy dipped a rag in a bucket of well water, wrung it out, and swabbed her head. Eight-year-old Gene ran for the midwife. Thirty minutes later Mrs. Brooks stormed through the open front door dripping wet, clutching her bag of miracles, instructing daddy to fit as many clean towels as he could in a pot filled with tears.

"Boil them in Borax then pull me a chair next to the bed. And see about those boys," she said, referring to my two other brothers playing nearby. "If I need you, I'll holler."

Two hours later, she hollered. "Robert, come meet your baby boy." Mrs. Brooks placed me in Daddy's calloused hands, careful not to disturb the tape holding down my umbilical cord. "Scrappy" she said. "Came out kicking and screaming."

Imagine Florida in August; hurricane season at its peak. Westerly winds off the African coast swirling beneath the floorboards. Mockingbirds whistling. Bullfrogs croaking from the muck. Rain dripping from the ceiling into big tin pans. Dusky light peeking through warped plywood banging against cracked windows. Children playing marbles. Laughing. Mrs. Brooks stirring a pot of salt pork and beans, singing old Negro spirituals. A newborn smacking at his mother's swollen breasts. Those were the sounds of our home in the woods. That is what daddy felt the day he vowed to buy the land.

Time moves through space like sawdust in the wind; here now, somewhere else later. Thirty months passed. The same midwife who brought four rough and tumblers into an expectant world delivered Anita Faye. Mama, though excited to finally have a baby girl, never ignored the rest of us.

A family of seven doing what families of seven do in six hundred square feet: sleep, eat, and pray. Barely room to breathe, Mama never had to tell us to go outside and play. Faye, Mama and Daddy slept in one bedroom. In another, four boys tossed and turned atop a sagging innerspring mattress, listening for things that go bump in the blackness.

Moments dispersed as dandelion seeds floating on the breath of spring. Summer lingered. School began. The alarm clock buzzed. Daddy showed up for another day's work at Lainhart & Potter, where he brought home scraps of lumber and building materials which we put to effective use.

In 1946 we added a front porch, a living room, dining room, and a third bedroom. The roof continued to leak. Most homes in the area had rooftops made of plywood or cheap yellow pine under roofing paper and shingles. But the only thing between me and the great beyond was layers of tar paper secured directly to the rafters and a rotted roof deck. It provided quick, inexpensive protection from the elements. That is, until a squall passed overhead tormenting tree limbs, violently ripping paper from roofing nails.

It wasn't uncommon for me to explore the celestial bodies dancing in the night sky through openings the size of footballs. From this unique vantage point, Buck taught me to recognize the Big and Little Dippers; Orion the hunter with its bright red star; Hydra, the sea serpent, as it stretched through the sky like a giant python. He taught me about the gravitational pull of the moon and sun and how they cause the oceans to rise and fall. Buck taught me this and more while we daydreamed in darkness.

Despite humble beginnings, Mama never allowed us to feel sorry for ourselves, where we lived, what we did or didn't have. "Be grateful you have a roof over your head and food on the table," she'd say. "Always hold your head high." Everything I've achieved in life is due to Mama's wisdom. She never talked down to us or made us feel unworthy. No, she told us we could be and do whatever we wanted in life.

Mama supported my dream of becoming a professional baseball player. She supplied me with instruction books and sports equipment, pep talks and hugs. She came to every game, celebrated every win, comforted me in loss. Some parents are around, but mama was present. She was the gift that kept on giving. She was the fortune in the land.

Our Garden of Eden

WE LIVED HIGH ON the hog. Seventy-five percent of our food came from the land. Out of the fertile, humid earth, sprung up every plant and tree good for soul and sustenance. In arm's reach grew bunches of banana and fig. Green mangoes we ate until our stomach swelled in pain; palm of Christ readied for use.

Mama made sweet jelly from an abundance of guava. Orange blossoms perfumed the air with goodness. A cherry hedge lined the driveway. We picked huckleberries and blueberries in the woods. Strawberries plumped with goodness ripened in nearby fields.

Our neighbor, Mr. Jones, grew acres of berries and vegetables. In the hush of moonlight's glimmer, Honeyman, Buck, and I creeped stealthily on our bellies between rows of tomatoes and sweet corn. Our mission was to arrive undetected beneath a cover crop of wheat and rye. When we made it safely to the queen of scarlet fruits we ate until plants were stripped bare. Mr. Jones thought blackbirds were robbing him blind when all along our stomachs were full of his berries. Little did we know at the time; Mr. Jones would have given us our fill of the crimson beauties had we only asked.

We raided fields of tubers by sticking our fingers into the cool earth, plucking out shirt loads of sweet potatoes. A deacon at the church grew an acre of watermelons big as piglets. As soon as we'd see him leave the house, we'd run across the lot, grab the biggest one we could carry, and run into woods. We'd smash the melon open on a sharp rock, scoop out the sweet flesh by hand, and bask in the glow of victory. The deacon saw a boy stealing his melons once and shot at him. The boy shot out of there so fast and never stole again. We raided fields untouched, until we understood our innocent fun was had at the hands of another man's toil.

Food was plentiful. It wasn't always what we wanted, but it was always available. Even still, if my brothers had something I didn't, I'd fit and fume. One day mama gave the three older boys two juicy oranges apiece; I got four lemons. Theirs's was much bigger than mine. Even though I had three to their two, for the life of me I couldn't understand why they got what seemed at the time a surplus.

There they sat, smug, chewing sweet sections of sunshine, juice sliding down their chins onto hairless chests. I felt like Charlie Brown who got a rock in his trick or treat bag.

"Mama," I said, tears streaming down my cheeks. "Why do they get oranges and I get lemons?"

"Well Danny," Mama said, hand on my shoulder. "You know what you have to do, right?"

"No Mama. Tell me what I have to do."

Barely school age, I didn't like being the youngest. The littlest meant scraps and hand-me-downs; first to see, last to get. It meant errand boy and broken toys and doing what I was told. I needed to figure out how to outsmart and outmaneuver.

"Tell me Mama," I asked again. "What must I do?"

"Well Danny. You get the biggest, prettiest jar you can find and fill it with water," she said. "Cut your lemons in half and squeeze 'em good into the water. Add sugar and stir."

"What then Mama?"

"You go sit under a shady tree, count your blessings, and enjoy your lemonade."

Worked like a charm; my brothers swarmed around me like thirsty mosquitoes. I didn't know it then, but Mama taught me a lesson that has served me well, most importantly to trust her wholeheartedly. Never did I question a word out of her mouth. She taught me life isn't always fair, but it's always redeemable.

I learned at a tender age how much I loved to win. Under the mango tree, lemonade in hand, I watched my brothers grovel at the bit. Won't lie; it felt good. I swallowed down my lemonade and basked in the shade of conceit.

Well, God don't like ugly. Three years later I cast a fishing line high into the tree trying to pull down green mangoes. It caught on a limb before I yanked it down into thick St. Augustine grass, got the iron hook lodged deep into my bare foot. I tried to pull it out but only made matters worse. I hooted and hollered thinking my baseball career was over before it began.

Daddy came home and found me hopping on one leg in pain. Without asking what happened, he pulled on the hook with a pair of rusted pliers, but the barb was lodged so deeply he couldn't get it.

"Danny," he said, holding my bloodied foot. "Got to run you to the hospital." Pine Ridge was the only medical facility in the county that treated Blacks. We didn't go often because Mama, using home remedies, did most of our doctoring. The practice of folk medicine is handed down by word of mouth from one generation to the next. This highly trusted system of curing diseases and promoting physical wellbeing was used to support blacks and poor whites. Traditional medicine failed to provide accessible care. Sometimes it wasn't worth the drive over the bridge. But they removed the hook, and we had to provide our own aftercare.

Mama boiled a cloth in Palm of Christ with rose apple vines and herbs from the garden, wrapped my foot to draw the poison out, and made me lay down. She changed the gauze every day for a week and I healed unblemished.

Another time I was congested and feverish. In those days, the theory was if you didn't get rid of the cold it would bring on the whooping cough or tuberculosis. Mama took me tight in her arms and sucked mucous out my nose until I breathed freely. I swallowed down three tablespoons of black draught, a purgative made of water, senna leaves, Epsom salts, ginger, and coriander. We'd run back and forth to the outhouse for hours.

I grew up in a time when Polio, a highly infectious virus, caused muscle weakness, paralysis and even death. It was a feared disease in the United States before a vaccine became available. The illness was once considered a "White disease," leaving many Black practitioners untrained in the recognition of symptoms. Many children went undiagnosed and untreated.

A five-year-old Faye complained that her legs were hurting badly while she and Mama were out shopping one day. Mama and Daddy rushed her to the doctors where she underwent a rudimentary exam. The doctor advised them to keep Faye away from other children and massage her legs with liniment just in case she had the polio. Give her a tonic of strychnine and let it run its course. Faye stayed with Grandma for more than a week before the doctors said it wasn't anything to worry about. She was fortunate. Many Black children suffered from the disease's crippling effects. Such was the way of life in the woods.

I'm glad there have been advances in science. Our doctors and nurses were some of the brightest but remained under-trained in medical advances. We had the universal Old Farmer's Almanac and folklore passed down through generations. However, the greatest medicine of all came from prayers and the biodiversity of the land.

The woods teemed with possum, rabbit, and coon; canals overflowed with snook and snapper. We had a yard full of chickens we raised for Harvey Barbeque, a Tamarind Avenue restaurant in West Palm Beach that people of every race and creed once visited. In return, we kept the brown eggs which we sold, and ate as many chickens as we wanted. Sometimes a hundred or more chickens scratched at the ground or squawked in the coop.

Before school, I scattered corn and set the hens. Daddy taught me the difference between cock and hen. "The rooster has long tail feathers and a red crown; the hen don't." When a rooster finds food, his hens eat first. A rooster protects his hen if she is threatened or attacked. Daddy was our rooster. He kept a rifle and shotgun at the ready.

On one occasion, as day darkened to night, Honeyman, Buck, and I played near the edge of the road, thinking the angry glow we noticed in the distance was the sun settling into the horizon. Moving closer, we saw clear across to Old Dixie a tall cross blazing in the sky. Mama saw it too because she motioned for us to come inside.

My age group was part of the "Silent Generation." We were expected to work hard, stay quiet, and never question authority. We learned early in life that Mama's demands were justified, so we ran into the house and she hid us under her long billowy housedress like a hen folds her chicks under wings. Daddy took his shot gun off the rack and stood on the front porch, mumbling Dagummits and dares.

"I wish they would come to my house and scare my wife and kids. I'll shoot 'em dead."

Mercifully, the grace of God appeared, and no one in white pointy hats, masks with eyeholes, and floor-length robes came near us. Never did my parents flinch. Ever. I witnessed courage under fire and vowed always protect my family. Daddy led the charge. No greater an example could he set.

Twice a year he and Granddad got down to serious business. It was time to slaughter hogs. They, with two or three other men, gutted, cleaned, and butchered pigs bigger than Daddy. Every part of the hog was saved: ears to intestines to feet, salt-cured and hung in the smoke house. We ate ham every Holiday.

Daddy was the farmer; I, the hired hand, earning fifty cents a month tilling an earth of plenty. Every year we started seedbeds and waited for shoots to appear. On bended knees, I sowed sprouts into furrows of organic matter of chicken manure and decomposed leaves. At harvest, twisted vines spilled over with okra, cucumbers, squash, and beans. Plump tomatoes dropped to the ground for the crows.

"Danny, get me a mess of greens and a handful of okra." Mama cooked Sunday dinners with love as the main ingredient: meatloaf, fresh vegetables, and rice. We regularly ate fried fish dinners with hoe cakes drenched in Alaga syrup, "the sweetness of the south." Daddy poured syrup on everything from chicken to yams. He cherished his Alaga syrup so much that he could have, like Hank Aaron and Willie Mays, advertised his love for the brand.

Under dusk's fiery glow, we piled into the car to survey the area along the banks; Mama and Daddy in the front, my brothers and I on the running board, Faye, and the family dog in the back. As soon as I'd spot something moving near the bank I'd point and yell, "Stop! There go one!" Shoot, let loose, retrieve: our formula for a good hunt. Gypsy was a faithful companion who loved her job of dropping the kill at our feet.

If you lived in the country, you had a dog. In fact, we had a lot of dogs, and we didn't discriminate. One of our firsts was a loyal white dog that Faye called Scottie. He rode in the backseat, rested his snout on the top of the front seat, and panted down Mama's neck. I can tell you Mama didn't like that.

We had a mixed breed German Shephard that chased the chickens around and ate eggs out the nests. When we took him hunting, instead of closing in on the kill, he scared them away, as if to warn "git!" Daddy, tired of the mutt not earning his keep, took him miles away in the dark of moonlight and left him in the thick of the forest. Crack of dawn the chickens squawked and clucked like a storm was about to roll in. Well, a storm did roll in. There sat the mutt, licking yolk off his mangy paws.

Two times again Daddy took him further into the woods, and each time the crazy dog made it back to the coop. Eventually, Daddy was won over. He kept the dog until it died, burying it at the wood's edge where the chickens scratched the earth foraging for grubs.

Two or three dogs later came a canine with panther-like fur and razor-sharp teeth who became a fast and faithful friend. Mama never allowed dogs in the house, but Dottie found her way in every night and slept at the foot of my bed snuggled next to a calico cat named Kitnik. I loved her, but in Mama's eyes, Dottie was Satan's wife. One day, as my one-year-old nephew played at my feet in the grass, Dottie, full of jealous rage, tried to bite him on the leg. Mama was so mad she grabbed the rifle. I pleaded with her, "Mama no. I'll keep her away from the baby." She didn't shoot the poor dog, but you best believe I never allowed Dottie near another small child.

Nature Boy proved to be Daddy's most faithful companion. They fished, hunted, and even picnicked together at the beach. They were inseparable. When Daddy first taught us how to shoot the rifle, Nature Boy was there. He lured rabbits from bushes by day. When we hunted in the dead of night, he was there to protect us from bobcats and bear. When Nature boy died, it was as if Daddy lost a limb. He cried for days.

Daddy, a sharpshooter, killed anything that jumped in the brush. Buck reigned supreme with a slingshot, able to knock a pigeon out a strangler fig a hundred feet away.

We frequently spread fish guts at the woods' periphery to attract racoon and possum, which was our main meal. In the calm of night, they'd creep out the tree hollow toward the bait. Gypsy stayed on high alert. She'd sniff out predators and wake us in the dead of night with a bark and muffled growl. I'd grab the flashlight and out the door we'd run. Buck killed the target before Daddy positioned his gun.

A shallow hole, layered with green palm leaves and heated coals, singed coon fur down to bare flesh. We'd wash, gut, and bring the coon to Mama where she'd boil and bake with sweet potatoes and red peppers from the garden. A meal fit for a king and his princes. Faye never liked the taste.

Mama warned us to beware the gators floating on the water's surface camouflaged as logs. Once, while out cutting firewood for the stove, Buck spotted a stick and mud nest where nearby a two hundred-pound gator sunned on the bank.

He catapulted a large round stone dead between the gator's eyes and knocked it out cold. We rushed over, cracked the axe over its head, and ate gator all year long.

"Stay out those waters. Nothing but trouble in there." Mama was not the worrisome type, but she didn't swim, and hated for us to play in or near the canal. Her words echoed true years later.

Seven, eight guys met after church each week to hang out at the canal to swim, especially during the warm weather months. A storm passed by a day before, leaving the water thick and murky with mirth.

Junior Morrison and friends jumped into the canal to cool off, swimming in and out of depths above their heads. An hour later, while everyone lay on the bank jiving around smoking Camels, someone asked a question that set off an instant panic.

"Hey, where's Junior?"

Two or three guys jumped in the water, cigarettes hanging from their mouths. Another ran to see if he had gone home. Yet another showed up at our front door yelling, "Honeyman! We can't find Junior Morrison!" He and Honeyman, close friends, rarely were seen without each other.

Honeyman shot out the house, raced eight blocks to the canal and jumped into a dismal unknown. He spent half an hour plunging up and down in the abyss. By now half the town was on the bank. Men jumped into the muddy water to search. So many people, so many hours, no Junior.

In the quiet of morning, a swollen body floated to the surface. Ruled an accident, Junior got caught in the undergrowth and was unable to free himself. Honeyman was torn up for weeks. The community mourned for months.

For Blacks, the sea sprays memories of a wretched, woeful past. Captured African men and women were transported by ship as goods to be bartered and sold. Crewmen sometimes drowned slaves at sea to conserve rations or to collect insurance for lost cargo. Many slaves killed themselves in defiance by sinking into the ocean willingly. It's a regrettable part of our history, and because of it, men and women of all races have tried to remedy the wrong.

Riviera Beach was a small town in the country; there wasn't much to do. You ran in the same circles; you did many of the same things. There were no more than twenty houses on the street. In fact, you had to walk at least a block to reach your neighbor. It was nothing but land and water.

Occasionally we ventured toward the shore. When I was ten, we'd go to market, gut the fish, and sell baskets full for seventy-five cents. To get where we were going, we'd pass by Burt Reynold's house. At the time, his father was assistant police chief, so it looked good for his family to blend with all the residents. We'd meet up and play on E avenue where most of the Conchs lived.

We were always happy to play with new blood. The conchs, alleged to have Black Bahamian blood, had no problem hanging with us. Every so often, a team of white kids joined us. We never had problems, but as their parents found out, they'd put a stop to it.

In 1949, there were only a handful of Black police officers under Chief Britt. Our officers couldn't go in the white areas and patrolled neighborhoods whose residents looked like them.

Senator Phil Lewis, state senator for ten years, moved from Chicago with Mission Company. He bought and cleared a lot of land in the black areas. In 1950 he donated land for Tate Park.

Three Fifths Less than Justice

SYLVIA WAS THE MIDDLE of five daughters born to Willie Ellis and Hanna Jones: Anna, Sadie, Marie, Sara. The sisters were unafraid to use their minds or dirty their hands. Mama shared with her sisters a long and proud heritage of self-sufficiency. Each was gifted in her own right, yet Grandma spoke repeatedly of mama's natural intelligence and her intense love of learning. Mama would have continued her education, but in those days, if you were pregnant, you got married.

Not particularly athletic or artistically inclined, Mama's gift to the world was her ability to always see the bright side, "consider it pure joy." She committed her way to the Lord, kept His word with a glad heart, and held few grudges despite income inequalities and employers who viewed her as less than human, regardless their noble intent.

Mama worked where she could. On occasion she split her week between day work in the Palm Beaches and her position at the port, too heavy a load for a righteous woman to carry. She stood on her feet ten hours every day for two years. When the barges and ships docked, Mama helped unload pounds of cargo. At the end of the day she lifted her burdens to the Lord. She never winced nor cried aloud; her head was bloodied but never bowed. By the time the baking position opened, her strength was renewed.

An outstanding cook, Mama got a baking job at the local Howard Johnson, becoming the hotel's first Black woman in that position. She spent nights, weekends, and holidays kneading and pounding dough, standing until her feet swelled like yeast rolls in a hot oven. It was a grueling job. She earned three fifths less than justice. Five dollars a week if lucky. Three dollars a week if descended from slaves. Don't complain. Be thankful for a job where you get to bring home old foods still good.

Mama refused to wear the face her employers expected: servile and desperate. With a husband and four boys she was never going to be hungry, alone, or afraid; that you can count on.

Daddy taught us to work, mama showed us how to cook, clean, sew, and ways to style Faye's hair. "I do not want you held captive to no woman," she told us.

Each night, Gene cooked, wrapped a plate of food in newspaper, placed it beside the kerosene lamp, and positioned mama's house shoes below the table's wooden edge. Mama would come home tired but undefeated. Before eating she prayed the exhausted Black woman's prayer: "Thank you, Lord." After supper, Buck brushed mama's curls, I rubbed her feet, Faye, reading aloud, sat cross-legged on the rug near the wood stove.

Three years on the job, mama finally would have off a holiday. Christmas. Our favorite. Turkey, ham, collards, and pies. Baseballs, bats, and pitchers' gloves. Marbles and checkers and roller-skates. Books enough for Faye. Argyle socks for Daddy. Fifty-cent eau de toilette for mama.

Two days before Christmas eve, the supervisor put mama back on the schedule.

"Ma'am, I am supposed to have the Holiday off this year," mama said. "You already approved my time."

"Mrs. Calloway I'm sorry. We had a scheduling conflict."

"But ma'am, I promised my three young children. Is there no one else to work?"

"Ms. Sylvia," she said. "You are on the schedule. It won't be changed again."

"Ma'am, I cannot disappoint my babies."

"Sylvia, if you have a problem, I expect you can leave right now."

I'm like mama in myriad ways, but in this one regard for sure: you can ask me to do anything, but don't you ever tell me what to do.

A meek, faithful servant of the Lord, mama first built up her house then trained me and my siblings in the way we should go. She implored us to trust in the Lord with all our heart, to not lean on our own understanding. By example she led. Mama taught us that your word is your bond. She had told us she was going to be home for the holiday and refused to go back on her word.

That moment, right then, mama breathed in the fullness of the Lord and stood on His promise that He would neither leave nor forsake her.

"Ma'am," mama said to her supervisor. "With all due respect then, I expect my week's pay. I quit."

Check in hand, mama sauntered out the hotel north on Belvedere Road, never to step foot through its doors again as an employee. Homeward bound; no more sweet treats and milk, day-old donuts and bread.

Spirit of the Wood

GRANDDAD DISTILLED ALCOHOL DEEP in the backwoods of Lee County Georgia. Corn mash, barley, and rye. Sometimes rotted scuppernongs and apples. Made moonshine, corn liquor. White lightning; clear and unaged. Bootlegged 80-proof spirits in mason jars and sturdy clay jugs. Keep the smoke low Joe; don't want to attract the law. Crossed county lines by day, dodged revenuers, and the Ku Klux Klan at night. Granddad was making money while chasing a dream.

A Black man under Jim Crow laws had no business pushing boundaries, especially with a wife and children at home. The deep south in early nineteen hundred demanded you keep your head low-slung, don't look the man in the eye, and act like you're too dumb to know better. Too many stories of blood coloring clay red and burnt skin striping the yellow poplar black. But not Granddad. He'd spit in your eye and talk about it later.

Granddad was a good storyteller, sharing cautionary tales about his misadventures in the woods and years spent running from the law. One memorable story involves an unsuspecting ten-year-old accomplice. Granddad asked him to keep watch; let him know if a stranger comes by. Whistle once if he's white, two if he's holding a gun.

While the boy played alone on the edge of the shadowy forest, a gangly, orange-bearded man approached riding a palomino quarter horse, chewing a fat cigar, cradling a Remington M8.

"Boy. Where's your pappy?" the man asked.

"Suh, I ain't got no pappy."

"You lying to me boy? Is he in them woods?"

"Nossuh. I ain't never told a lie. Nothin' in them woods but strange fruit and ghosts."

"Well, you tell that nigra I'm looking for him, hear?"

"Yassuh. If I see that nigra, I'm gonna say you is looking for him."

As soon as the man was out of sight, the boy wet his lips, puckered, placed his tongue on the roof of his mouth and blew. Nothing. Tried to whistle twice. Nothing again, so he high-tailed barefoot over felled pines and sweet-gum burrs shouting, "Mister! Mister! A white man with a gun is hunting you down."

No questions asked, Granddad grabbed the boy by the hand and ran like the dickens toward safety, finding sweet refuge in the forest's bosom. He stuck a half-dollar coin in the boy's clammy palm and sent him on his way. Never again was the boy seen playing unshod and carefree on the outskirts of the woods.

As Granddad made his way back to town, the orange-bearded revenuer caught sight of him, cocked his rifle and started shooting. He ducked and dodged bullets and ran back into the woods, confident the revenuer would lag for fear a ghost might unmercifully haunt him in his sleep.

As much as I liked Granddad's stories, I never liked nor uttered the N-word. For me, the N-word is a painful reminder of oppressive injustices wrought at the hands of men and women who considered us uncivilized and inferior. Animals. Cargo. Regrettably, it is an ugly part of American history. But, to erase a piece of history simply because it is an uncomfortable reminder is like cutting your toe off because you got a deep splinter from the floorboards.

Black men bear some responsibility for their role in the word's misuse. There are better ways to endear oneself to another without using derogatory patois that borders on self-hate and contempt for one's ancestry. We may be the only culture that uses denigration as adoration.

Six decades spent working with youth of all races and ethnicities, and still, less than six decades ago laws existed that set out to marginalize and repress "Colored folk." Unfortunately, we once again find ourselves at a similar crossroad in history, when hateful rhetoric is spewed from both sides of the aisle. When will we learn that hate fuels divisions? Soon, it is them against us, then us against the world. Martin Luther King Jr., one of the greatest orators of all time wrote: "Hate cannot drive out hate; only love can do that."

To use such a demoralizing word about myself would be madness. And I love you too much to use vilification to communicate comradery. I'd rather use the word "brother" as a term of endearment rather than utter a word that maligns our manhood. Should we continue to foolishly embrace the false pride associated with such dehumanizing figures of speech, i.e., ho, bitch, niggah, or do we finally understand the harm such offensive words cause? When do we stop adding insult to injury? These are questions we must answer if, as MLK hoped, we are to be judged by the content of our character rather than the color of our skin.

Granddad managed to escape harm from the KKK and revenuers on the run from Leesburg to Riviera and all points between, but he didn't give up the life. The family settled in a small home on Silver Beach Road, just south of the scrubland and backwoods; ample cover for his illicit activities. Like many other men, white and Black alike, he bootlegged throughout the days of the Great Depression. He thought there was no other way to make a living that allowed him to support a wife and five daughters in the style in which he was accustomed.

In his backyard he built a smoke house and planted all sorts of fruit trees, ornamentals, and flowers. The grounds, replete with splendor, was a proverbial Shangri-La. Granddad became a prolific gardener, cruising over the Flagler bridge in a brand-new Chrysler to beautify the lawns of Palm Beach mansions. Thank God he spared Mama from a life she did not deserve.

Honestly, Mama's father was a scoundrel: reckless with words, women, and whiskey. Turns out Granddad had paved an inconspicuous path through his garden straight to another woman's house. I don't know if Grandma ever knew about the mistress. Back then, women either didn't know, didn't care, or did something about it though I doubt it was the latter.

I do know Riviera was a small town. Barely five hundred people. Everybody knew somebody and most Blacks ran in the same circles. When Grandma died from complications of a stroke, Granddad married the woman who lived on the edge where the morning sun kissed the grove. Mama and her sisters didn't acknowledge Granddad's new lady, calling it foul of him to cheat on their mother while she was in compromised health.

Providence is sometimes cruel. Sylvia means Goddess of the forest, *Silva*, Spirit of the wood. What an ironic twist of fate. Mama never cussed, smoked, or drank, but turns out she had more in common with Granddad than once thought. Her appreciation of tropical foliage and gardening in midlife was either an homage to her father or a matter of the coconut not falling far from the tree. Sadly, she never warmed to him.

When Granddad came up in age, he named me in his will and testament as executor of his estate. Savings, house, possessions were for me to do with as I pleased. Mama wasn't happy about that. She wanted nothing from him, but she didn't want any problems with her sisters either.

"Danny, put Sara's name on the will," she told me. "I don't want your aunts thinking I will benefit just because you are in charge."

"Mama, Granddad don't have nothing worth anything."

"Danny, I don't care. Do as I say."

When Granddad died in 1992, he had long outrun the revenuers and patiently outlived two wives. He had a two hundred fifty-dollar Gulf Life insurance policy, which, at the time bought, was enough to bury him. Forty years later it wasn't worth the paper it was printed on. We left the house to Aunt Sara.

Mama and her four sisters gathered around the mahogany dining room table. An English sideboard revealed good times of days past. Inside the middle compartment sat two corn liquor filled mason jars and an old pipe.

"The funeral and burial cost twenty-six hundred dollars," I said. "That's only five hundred twenty dollars apiece; I got mama's share."

Aunt Sadie's part was coming out of my pocket too, but nobody had to know that. She put aside her grievance with Granddad and unselfishly cared for him as his health declined.

By now you've heard that when it comes time to put up, people often shut up or disappear. Fond as I was of my aunts, they would have run for the hills if given the chance.

"I don't have it," one said.

"Me neither," said another.

Mind you, each was well-cared for in life. In fact, the first one to cry broke had recently gathered her savings from the innards of her Sterns & Foster to finally deposit close to forty thousand dollars in a bank account.

Anyhow, I paid for the funeral. Granddad was laid to rest among towering conifers and woodland sprites. Sylvia Mae never spoke of him again.

The Old-Timer

DADDY WAS PROUD AND ornery but there was nothing he wouldn't do for his family. He worked day and night to prove, if only to himself, that life hadn't passed him by. When he didn't haul lumber or paint, he spent time with us.

Often, we'd go to a vacant stretch of sea grape covered sand and brush on Singer Island where the clearest, coolest water kissed the coast. This was our shore, turned black by the laws of the land. Out there, staring where ocean melted into sky blue, and silver fish leapt on soft ripples, time stood still. Dreams were welcomed here. Simply toss desires onto white capped waves and wait for hightide to wash them ashore like dollars well-spent. No wonder Daddy loved it here; he was free to cast his dreams in the wake.

If fish could talk, they'd speak full of soul and sorrow about an old timer from Leesburg, Georgia who feared no myth or man. He received an inheritance of courage by his father who worked the land. His land. Acres, a horse, and a mule. His father taught him a job pays dividends when done well and money spent on wine and women is unwise. Daddy was a dutiful son, and he took his father's teachings to heart. Pennywise and hungry, Daddy did what he had to do.

Many a dusk and a dawn we'd drive to the old timber and steel bridge to cast reel and rod into the inlet from the crumbling floor of the fishing pier. The floorboards bounced so much I thought we'd fall through into the brackish water below. The northern winds brought blue fish and mackerel; catfish scavenged yearlong. Some days we'd have buckets of fish to sell at market for a quarter a piece. Other days we'd spend on the greens, caddying, but unable to play. Every penny counted, and Mama counted every penny.

The minimum wage in 1940 was thirty cents an hour. White men averaged just under a thousand dollars per year, while the average Black man in the south earned about three hundred. Census records from that same year showed Robert Calloway Sr earned five hundred dollars, just under the mean annual income for Black men nationwide. Daddy had the third highest reported income in Palm Beach County's expanding Precinct #3 "colored settlement." Five hundred dollars was all the money in the world for a laborer with a fourth-grade education. Poor by today's standards, we were one of the richest families in the neighborhood because of the values Mama and Daddy instilled in us.

Sadly, Daddy had to work ten times harder just to make three times less. A harsher truth is that eight decades later pay disparities still exist in the land of the free, where declared all men were created equal. When Thomas Jefferson wrote that the Creator endowed all men with certain unalienable rights, he must not have meant we who have "black complexions and fleecy locks." Inequalities must be addressed head on so future generations can thrive in a fair society. These are the self-evident truths for which I've advocated for the past sixty years.

You can bet the amount documented on the census didn't include mama's wages from day work or the couple cents Gene made hauling dirt and gutting fish. Every single penny earned went somewhere for something. Bird of paradise and crotons for the lawn, gas for the car, paint for the house, sports equipment for me. Chicks in the yard, vegetables in the garden; whatever we had was because Daddy worked for us to have it. He hustled for a dime of pride.

Daddy had a PhD in Streetology and a flare for fashion. He was another Black man with a dollar and a dream. He'd strut in the pool halls and jukes, not for liquor and women, but to hustle someone on the pool table.

Cheeky Robert was his name, sinking eight-balls was his claim to fame. Daddy ran the table with the same skill and creativity as his golf game. Billiards was much like golf: stance, grip, stroke. It's no wonder he played so well. He was a beast.

He usually left the poolhall double his money, handing his winnings over to Mama, who'd roll the grubby bills in a handkerchief and stick it in her bosom. When I traveled for games, she'd pull a couple dollars from the deep beyond and say, "I don't ever want you to go somewhere and can't get back to me." She wasn't going to depend on us to thumb a ride to get a ride. I need you to get home. "I'll never sleep until you are in this house, I don't care if it's five o'clock in the morning."

She said the same thing when I returned from the army. I used to laugh and ask, "Mama, I been all over the world. What were you doing then?"

"I put you in God's able hands," she said. "But it doesn't matter, when you're under this roof, I'm not gonna sleep until you walk through these doors." She told me I'd never understand what she was saying because I was a man. "I don't care how old you get, you're still my boy."

Mama was well up in age before she took her money out her bra and put it in First Marine bank, later known as Bank of America. But Daddy and Mama always believed in a rainy-day fund. No matter how much they made or didn't make, they kept at all times at least two hundred fifty dollars in their box at the Lake Park post office. They had a mailbox for mail and a safety deposit box for money and policies. One thing is for sure, Mama knew how to govern the money and Daddy knew how to make it, some kind of way.

An egomaniac, he had the little man syndrome and tried to make up for it by looking like a million dollars. Whenever the carnival was in town, he'd dress up and drive us there for games and rides. Of course, I won prizes for shooting baskets, while Buck and Faye spun on Ferris wheel seats hanging downward.

Meanwhile, Daddy thought he could outhustle a hustler. He had eighty dollars to bring home to Mama, earnings from a good week of caddying, playing billiards, and selling fish. But he wanted to double his money so he sat down to play three card monte, a game of quiet desperation in which a fool is fooled into betting his pay, thinking he can find the "money card" among three face-down cards. Well, Daddy soon lost his eighty dollars. Horror of horrors, he had to go home and tell Mama.

Daddy got home and broke down in front of us; cried the river Jordan, worrying about what would happen if he wasn't able to feed his kids. Mama reacted with little emotion. At ten years of age I watched him cry. I saw my Daddy in his weakest moment and vowed never to fall so low as to cry over something I could avoid. He beat himself up for years, but never gambled again.

Former Florida state Senator Phil Lewis and his family's Mission Company was one of Daddy's earliest employers. As foreman, he supervised the clearing of thousands of acres of land in Riviera Beach.

Buck and I had a weekend hustle working for Daddy passing out tickets to drivers. When trucks hauled debris to landfills, Buck handled the trucks going out, I gave tickets to the ones coming in. The men were paid by the truckload. At the end of the day, drivers turned in their tickets for pay.

The Senator's father, Frank J. Lewis, tendered land for a baseball park in the black section of town. I was the lead-off pitcher in the park's opening game. Prior to his generous donation, we played on a water-run sandlot with old shirts for bases.

When Daddy was laid off or there was downtime, to stay on the payroll he showed up to 111 North County Road to help the Senator and his wife Maryellen with their nine children.

Buck and I washed their two big Cadillacs every other week for a crisp twenty-dollar bill to split. When Daddy brought the Senator's boys to our home, we played games together and drank out the same soda bottles. Kids don't see color until somebody points it out.

Later in life, Senator Lewis treated me as well as anyone outside of my family has ever treated me. In fact, he was the first white man for which I had a mutual relationship. He stayed in touch with me as my careers evolved. He allowed me to stay in his Tallahassee apartment when I was there on business. We played golf on the weekends and with Dr. Easey and Herman, went to breakfast every other week. He was a man to be admired and emulated.

In July 2012, The Senator Philip D. Lewis Center opened, two months before he passed away. The resource center is for the county's homeless, acting as a midway point of access to services for those seeking to end their homelessness. What a wonderful legacy to leave in the county where he touched so many lives.

Still, more needs to be done. Under the bridge right now there are hungry and homeless people. Palm Beach County has over two hundred thousand hungry citizens trying to survive. How in the world are that many people starving when we are this close to Palm Beach? That makes no sense.

Daddy loved his job with the Mission Company over all others. He was treated with dignity and respect. He loved talking about sports so he could bring me into the conversation. When I started playing with the men at fourteen, Daddy viewed me as the greatest thing that ever happened to him. "Just look at my Danny." Then he'd pull a yellowed newspaper clipping from his wallet. "The Cubs are scouting my boy," he'd say proudly.

I appreciated Daddy's support. That's one reason I didn't mind helping him around the house. He worked so much it seemed a special treat to have him home. Some days his driving job took him north. He'd leave on Friday not seen again for three and four days. It felt like the 4th of July when he returned.

Every summer since the age of eight I helped lay new tar paper on the roof and gave the house a fresh coat of paint. Mixed equal parts white paint and water in a five-gallon bucket and stroked away. Gone was the weathered gray like the other houses; ours was white as spilt milk on freshly varnished floors.

Children used to tease us because at the time we had the only painted house, a black '26 Plymouth, and a perfectly cut carpet of green grass. We knew to cut it exactly right or we'd never hear the end of Daddy's wrath.

"You cut it too low...missed a spot...didn't clean the blades."

We learned quickly to do it right so we wouldn't have to do it over. Plus, we didn't want to hear Daddy's mouth. He was like a fingernail on a chalkboard.

We kept the Plymouth until Daddy bought a brand new 1954 green Chevrolet Bel Air complete with toothy grill and matching Continental kit. When he added a pink and gray sun visor it set it off with enviable distinction. Daddy was the first Black person in town to have a car so sophisticated. It was a big deal. Everyone wanted a ride in that beauty.

"Y'all smell like white folk. Think you better'n us," the kids would say.

Daddy said, "Ignore them Danny. Pay them no mind."

Growing up, I was ready to battle at the slightest provocation. I didn't intentionally seek out trouble; didn't avoid it either. Nevertheless, to a hotheaded eight-year-old, those were fighting words. Don't you ever say or do anything against me or my family or else there'd be hell to pay to strangers.

My passion gets easily confused with conceit; my tears with fear. In fact, most times when I cried as a boy it was because I was either really mad or trying to get out of trouble. Sometimes I think my punishments were used as a way to let me know who was boss. When I was fuming or just an insufferable tattletale, Daddy gave me chores, made me stay in the house, or took away my marbles. But they each spanked me one time and one time only.

Mama often read to us near the light of the kerosene lamp. Faye, Buck, and I, as was our custom, took turns brushing her hair as she read us bible stories or went over our lessons. It only took ten minutes before boredom set in. Reckless play led to a knocked-over lamp, which caused the curtain to catch fire. Faye stood there crying while I grabbed the afghan from the back of the settee and tried to smother the flames. Buck ran to the pump and filled a pail with water. Mama doused the flames, scolded us, and sent us to bed early as a punishment.

Daddy came home and smelled smoke. "Sib, something burning?"

"Yes, but I took care of it." No matter the circumstance, Mama managed to stay cool as an ocean's breeze. She taught us even if a tempest is brewing on the inside, put on a face of calm; keep the other person guessing.

Dissatisfied with the short answer Daddy asked again. "Well what happened Sib?"

"The lamp fell over and scorched the curtain is all."

"Is all? The damn house could have burnt down! Where them boys?"

"Leave them be," Mama said firmly. "Accidents happen."

"Welp, guess I got two chickens to skin in the morning."

When the cock crowed at dawn, Daddy was standing in the bedroom doorway rubbing his eyes. "Go cut me a switch off the tree."

Buck trudged out back, stripped a palmetto limb, and took the first few licks like he was having an out-of-body experience. Daddy kept switching Buck until he cried out in fits and starts. When I heard him whimpering like an injured puppy I went into a silent rage; blood boiled under my skin like a cauldron of hot oil on an open fire. Daddy turned to me and snapped the palmetto blade across my leg. As he lifted his arm to lash me again, I snatched the switch from his hand and thrashed him across the leg with it.

"Boy! Have you lost your ever-loving mind?"

Daddy stood for a moment in shock. Before I realized the stupidity of my actions, Daddy had already dragged me by the collar down the back stoop, strung me upside-down on the clothesline, and whipped the hell out of me. There I hung about half an hour before dropping to the ground. A nine-year-old boy hitting his father borders on lunacy. Don't do it.

Daddy never beat me again and I never gave him another reason to do so. I took a good butt whipping that day but learned my lesson. Honor your father and mother. You'll spare yourself a lot of grief if you follow that basic rule.

Still mobile, Daddy went here and there, sometimes popping up like a bad penny, but I always knew where he was and what he was doing. In time, I became responsible for the household expenses which freed him up for leisurely activities. He loved baseball and often watched the pros train during camp early in the year. But golf was always his first love, caddying regularly for Arnold Palmer and Gracie Emery.

Actually, Daddy would have made a good athlete. He had a natural propensity for the game which kept him playing even after he took ill. Prior to integration, he could only play during the last month of the season or in the evenings. After golf courses integrated, he made lasting friendships with players of every race.

Daddy was sometimes a fair-weather friend, especially with us. He might pal it up with us one minute and shoot us down the next. My love of golf began the moment Daddy put a club in my hand. He was a good golfer and taught me everything he knew, but I became a formidable rival as I honed my skills.

42

Eventually, student became master and I won most matches. It was not until I began beating Daddy that I realized where my hatred for losing originated. Daddy was a bad sport who hung his lip so low so often I stopped playing with him, tired of his endless grumblings. If this is how I behaved when I lost, its no wonder Mama threatened to pull me from teams.

Needing fresh blood, he took his teenaged grandsons, Darryl, and Ray up to the course. The boys were well-trained in the fundamentals of the game, and they grew into talented players. They played eighteen holes and beat Daddy so bad it was embarrassing. On the way home they laughed and teased him. "Granddaddy Rob, we got you this time." They were poking innocent fun, but Daddy didn't like it.

"You mannish devils, get out my car!" He screeched to a halt in the middle of a dark road seven miles from home. "And take your bags too!"

Darryl and Ray shouldered their bags and got to stepping. Daddy drove past yelling, "And you best not cry!"

Mama had prepared dinner for the three of them. It was late and she grew concerned they hadn't gotten home yet. When Daddy walked through the door alone, she asked, "Rob, where the boys?"

"I put them out the car."

"Out the car where Robert?"

"Up there in Jupiter. Teased me because they won the round. You think they are staying in my car after that?"

Two hours later the boys showed up on my doorstep dripping in sweat, barely standing. I fixed them something to eat as they told me what had happened.

"Welp," I said. "Guess you won't do that again."

What had Happened Was

GENE IS THE ONLY person beside Mama and Daddy to ever beat me. Eight years old and I was a tattletale. Daddy kept a rifle and a shotgun high on a rack, and he forbade us to touch them. Gene and Honeyman decide to take the rifle down and go hunting. Out all day and the only thing they killed was a red bellied woodpecker foraging on a dead Florida pine. Everybody knows you can't eat a bird that small. Instead of throwing it in the marsh or burying it, they foolishly threw it under the house.

Three days later Daddy came home from work and asked, "Danny, what in the world is smelling so bad?" He went room to room sniffing like a beagle. "Go look under the house and see if a chicken done scrambled there and died."

It was only natural he'd tell me to check since it was my job to feed and set the hens. "Oh no Daddy, it ain't a chicken. I know what is smelling so bad." Never one to pass on a good snitch, I couldn't wait to tell on Gene and Honeyman. Daddy had promised me a quarter if I kept an eye on things while he was gone.

"Well boy what is it?" Daddy grew angrier than a storm at sea. Gypsy whimpered and scampered backward out the room. Dogs are smart that way.

"It ain't no chicken. That's the woodpecker they killed."

"Who killed the woodpecker Danny?"

"Junior and Honeyman. They went hunting with that gun you told us to never touch."

"What you say boy?"

"Junior and Honeyman killed the woodpecker with the rifle and threw the bird under the house."

The four corners of our house stood on stacked cinder blocks. A blind man could see front to back. Tropical storms left one side teetering dangerously off-kilter. Still, like daddy, it endured.

"There it is Danny. Bag it up."

"Aww Daddy. Why don't Honeyman have to get it?"

"Did I ask you a question boy?"

"No sir." I wriggled under the house and wrapped the pecker up. Daddy handed me a quarter and said, "You done good son." Junior and Honeyman came home a few hours later. You could hear them a block away screeching like a barn owl in the night.

When Daddy went to work the next day, Junior vowed to make me sorry for snitching on him. He grabbed mama's long-handled brush and beat me silly. Buck, sensing a tempest brewing said, "Junior, stop hitting him!" But he persisted.

By now I was a fuming smoke stack. Pulling away, I climbed atop a stool, hoisted Daddy's .22 off the wall rack, and pointed it straight at Junior.

Honeyman yelled, "Boy, put that gun down."

Buck screamed, "Junior, I told you to leave him alone!"

46

By now Buck and Honeyman were in a state of panic. Junior stood there laughing. "Oh, he ain't gonna do nothing. He can't even cock the damn thing."

I supported the rifle with my elbows pressed in tight to my body, pointed the barrel toward Gene and inhaled. Holding the handgrip, I placed the rifle firmly against the muscle just inside my armpit and shoulder. Then, I leaned my head, let my cheek rest against the butt of the rifle, and put my finger on the trigger.

"Little brother," Buck said. "Please put that gun down."

When Honeyman saw I knew what I was doing he got so scared he hit the barrel of the gun. He didn't knock it out my hand, but the sheer force of the whack caused a bullet to shoot out between Junior's legs. Everyone froze. Was he dead or alive? Gene frantically ran his hands over his privates, making sure he didn't lose his manhood. When he realized he wasn't dead, he sighed a sigh of relief and charged at me again.

"I'm gonna kill you boy!"

"You ain't gonna do no such thing; I'm not scared of you." Confident their terror reign had ended I said, "You touch me, and I'll tell on you again." Honestly, I was more interested in putting another quarter in my pocket. Nonetheless, it took every bit of strength for Honeyman and Buck to hold Gene down.

"Told you to leave him alone." Buck cried hysterically, upset the situation had gotten so out of control. "Y'all need to get right with the Lord."

Honeyman snickered, shook his head, and said, "Dang boy; you a crazy fool."

Junior and I had no more problems the rest of his life.

Disdain for beatings grew as I entered puberty. I refused to become a scout, even though Gene, Honeyman, and Buck had each taken the oath:

On my honor, I will do my best. To do my duty to God and my country and to obey the Scout Law; To help other people at all times; To keep myself physically strong, mentally awake, and morally straight.

The oath wasn't the problem. In fact—and I didn't know it at the time—it perfectly expressed a personal code of conduct to which I've adhered throughout my life. No, the reason I stayed out was because of what Honeyman told me:

"You know if you break the rules you have to go through the line. We'll tear your ass up with the scout belt."

"Welp, guess I won't be a scout," I said. "Don't matter though. I'd rather play ball."

After I almost killed Gene, Daddy hid the guns away for a while. A few months passed before he let his guard down and returned them to their rightful spot on the rack. He issued the same warning: "Don't you boys touch them guns, you hear?"

Well, two years later Honeyman, who knew good and well he shouldn't handle the gun, decides to go hunting. He pulled the rifle from the rack and said, "Y'all come on. We're going to hang out at Streamline's."

"Don't touch that gun," Buck said. "We're gonna get in trouble."

"Boy, stop being a crybaby and grab Danny."

We'd get in as much trouble for not listening to the oldest in charge than for doing something wrong, so I snatched a glove and ball and headed down the road behind Honeyman, who had Daddy's rifle suspended over his shoulder. No sooner had we gotten to Streamline's, Honeyman disappeared into the woods.

Mr. and Mrs. Pierce were at work. Back then, the rule in most households was no parents, no company. Play outside or stay home, but don't you dare go inside. Fights break out. Things break and spill. Boys and girls play doctor and nurse. Teenagers mess around. Nine months later you're welcoming a new family member.

Outside, we slugged balls into trees, interrupting the cicadas deafening drone; catapulted rocks from slingshots, chased rabbits hither and thither. Streamline sweat like a hog in heat.

"Y'all come get some lemonade," he said. "Looks like rain."

Before long, Honeyman, gun in hand, peeked through the window. "Time to go kiddies."

Buck stuck his head out the unscreened window. "Hey man; give us a minute. We're 'bout to play marbles."

"We got to get back before Daddy," Honeyman said.

"Told you not to take that gun," Buck teased. "Daddy's gonna whoop your butt."

Streamline and I stood ten feet from the front door drawing a big circle in the dirt. Storm clouds loomed just above our heads; air so thick it oozed. A murder of crows rushed by cawing.

Then, something so unsettling happened that seventy years later it still makes me shake my head if I think about it. Buck leaned chest high out the window, grabbed the rifle by the barrel and Honeyman shoved it deep into his mouth. I don't know what ran through Honeyman's crazy head, but he looked Buck dead in the eye and pulled the trigger.

Good God Almighty! We ran into the house expecting to see Buck's brain splattered across Mrs. Pierce's blue brocade couch. Instead, the fool lay curled on the floor laughing his head off.

Streamline was either amused or relieved his mama wouldn't find out he had company in the house, but he wanted to do the same thing. His baby cousins stood by and laughed. I laughed. Buck rose from the dead. Honeyman passed the rifle to his left. Streamline reached for the barrel and it slipped from his hand. The butt hit the floor and up jumped the devil! A bullet shot through the barrel straight through Streamline's neck just missing his jugular vein.

"Oh my God you done shot him," Streamline's eight-year-old cousin screamed. Everybody screamed; we all screamed for ice cream. We were scared out of our minds. Blood squirted from his neck drenching everything red. Everywhere you looked was blood. Honeyman put his hand over the hole in Streamline's neck and blood oozed through his fingers.

"I'm going to get Mrs. McGaney!" She was the only one I could think of who had a car.

"Danny, you can't do that," Honeyman shouted. "The police gonna put me in jail." He just cried and cried. I never seen a man look so pitiful.

Buck said, "Yeah, Danny. They gonna put him in jail."

Streamline was standing there bleeding to death screaming at fever pitch and all they thought about was Honeyman going to jail. Unbelievable.

"Buck, go get the liniment!" Honeyman yelled.

Honeyman poured the liniment on the neck and Streamline nearly torpedoed through the roof. By now the boy was about to go into shock.

"What we gonna do, Honeyman?" There had to be something I could do. Mama worked at the port unloading exotic fruit off the ships. She often sent bunches of bananas to the Pierce's because she knew how much Streamline liked them.

"Get some bananas!" I knew that would calm him down. Yes, that had to work. "Streamline likes bananas!"

Buck ran from the kitchen with a bunch of green bananas and we start stuffing them down Streamline's throat. As soon as he swallowed them, we'd stuff more in his mouth. Good Lord, if he didn't die from his injuries, he would surely choke to death. As it was, he was about to pass out. We wrapped a cloth around his neck and put him in his bed. Mrs. McGaney, Streamline's aunt, showed up at the door; must have heard us screaming two blocks away. She rushed Streamline to the hospital. By the grace of God, he lived. Everybody was sick over what happened. Mama and Daddy were too upset to punish us. They knew we had to live with what had happened. That was punishment enough.

Buck should have died. Streamline could have died. When you see enough of these incidents, you either grow numb, or you realize how fragile life is and how important it is to follow the rules.

Fumbling Around

AFTER THE CLUB INCIDENTS Mama was wary of Honeyman and Gene taking me around trouble. Instead, we started hanging out at girls' houses when their parents worked. We had no problem finding willing takers; Gene simply dangled me as bait. Mama taught me about the birds and the bees, but my three brothers showed me where to find the honey.

I had barely gone through puberty when my brothers pushed me to have my first relations. My only experience previously was an innocent tongue kiss with the prettiest girl in town, Delores Webster. Our mothers, close friends, were pregnant at the same time. They daydreamed of one having a boy, the other a girl who would marry and give them beautiful grandchildren.

In May we had an event called plait the maypole. During these field day events, it was normal for boys and girls to sneak into the woods and kiss. Friends asked, "Did you get some tongue?" French kissing was an important rite of passage for young boys. Leave a juvenile to his or her own devices and often they will spin out of control. Me, I was a painted Duncan yoyo wrapped around my brother's finger.

One day Mama asked me. "Danny. Are you out there messing around with those little girls?"

"No ma'am," I said, lying through my teeth. Couldn't tell mama her fourteen-year-old baby's been sleeping around. It was bad enough I told Faye. She needed to know how smooth operators like me got the girls and that boys would try to do to her exactly what I was doing to their sisters. In fact, I was messing with some of Faye's friends and she didn't like it. "Mama tell Danny not to bother my girlfriends." I told Faye if she washed my dishes, I'd leave her friends alone. She washed them and I left them alone, not because of our pact but because I wasn't interested in them all along. They weren't my type.

Very annoyed at my one-sided talk, Mama said to me, "Boy, you always talking about the pretty girls. Stop being so beauty struck."

"Mama, I have to have a pretty girl on this arm."

"Danny, beauty is only skin deep."

I got smart-mouthed and said, "Well mama, ugly goes to the bone."

Daddy laughed like a schoolboy. "You tell em my boy. I don't want no ugly grandbabies."

A few sleepless years later I learned that dishonesty leaves a mark on your conscience, if it doesn't first stab you in the heart. Some people can lie with a straight face, go about their business.

Me, I was burning feverishly with guilt before I admitted to mama that I was having sex regularly. One too many relations led to many more, I got sick and had to go to the doctors. Mama sat with me in the office waiting on the diagnosis. I would have fallen to the floor in shame if the doctor had told me I had a venereal disease. Instead, he said I was oversexed.

"Danny's been a bad boy," the doctor said.

"You not telling me something I don't already know," Mama said, eying me with such disappointment I vowed never to lie to her again.

"Daniel, when's the last time you've had sex?"

I was already embarrassed that Mama had to hear this, but I wasn't going to lie to her again. "Day before yesterday."

"And how many times in the past week."

Now I 'm counting in my mind how many times I snuck and snaked in the back seat of the car at the park with a different girl over the past week.

"Uh, every day."

Mama was embarrassed and I was embarrassed for her. I don't know how or when things had turned but I didn't want to lose Mama's support. It meant too much to me. "Mama, I'm sorry."

"Beat up some eggs, milk, and nutmeg; make him sip it for ten days," the doctor told mama. "That'll clear him up good."

Back then, penicillin was secondary to liniments, tonics, and folk medicine. I've swallowed more homemade concoctions than I'd care to remember. Some are worth their weight in gold, others are poison, no matter what you cut it with. Regardless, there existed no wonder drug for lying. I bore the wrath of shame for a long time.

We were out sneaking around with the neighborhood girls and Mama knew it. A mother's intuition can sniff out lies like a hound tracking a rabbit. Years earlier she sat the four of us down and said, "I don't want no mother and father coming here saying one of my sons has to marry their daughter." In the olden days, if you made a girl pregnant, you had a shotgun wedding.

"Listen to me," she said, handing us each a box of rubbers. "Keep these on the night table and use them when you need to."

Mama didn't mince words. She spoke softly and confidently, with a tenderness dissimilar to Daddy's gruff and overbearing nature. It was normal for him to pluck the same string for days. That's one reason we kept our shenanigans—around him anyway—to a minimum; we didn't want to hear his mouth.

Mama became my confidante; I shared everything with her. I couldn't get anything past her anyway. There was nothing we couldn't cry over or laugh about. Over the years Mama became everything to me. I honored her without reserve. Everybody on the streets knew that Dan Shamrock Calloway didn't play if he heard you say something about his sister or his mother.

I never played the dozen, a game where you joke about somebody's mama. "Your mama's so ugly..." I didn't play that. I will not say anything against anybody's mother, and I will not allow anybody to say something negative about mine. That is where I draw the line.

Long ago my eyesight failed, but in my mind's eye I see Mama as if she were standing before me, chocolate eyes twinkling beneath wire-rimmed glasses, lips curled upward toward heaven, arthritic hands clasped in supplication. By faith was I saved. The fervent prayers of a righteous woman saved me.

Drunker than Cooter Brown

GONE TWO THIRDS THE day, Daddy made men out of us in a hurry. In his absence we had to take care of Mama, the house, and one another. We didn't poop or piss without the other knowing. The oldest child was supposed to look after his younger siblings without lips poked out in protest.

Mama didn't allow my brothers to go anywhere without me. "If you can't take your little brother, then you can't go," she'd say. So, I'd tag along with them to the juke joint where we slurped ice cream, danced, and flirted with pretty girls. I was like a linchpin around their necks. For a ten-year-old scamp it was a euphoric experience. Buck didn't like it. He knew wherever there's liquor, there's trouble.

One day the club owner hurled a cue ball at a man running toward the door for reasons unknow. I don't know if the man was skipping out on his tab, or if he was being chased. Anyway, he missed his target and hit an innocent man in the temple, busting his skull wide open. It took two days for an ambulance to come for him. He died.

My Uncle, a six foot six, two hundred fifty-pound man got drunk on payday. He didn't drink during the week but every Friday he stopped by the juke and drank until he slunk over like a ripe drupe. Every Friday, my aunt walked down the dirt road, woke us up and said, "Boys, go get your uncle and bring him home." Imagine me, a scrawny ten-year-old, with Buck and Honeyman trying to carry home a man as big as Goliath the Gittite. The very sight of a slobbering grown man who peed himself did more for me than anything else to deter me from drinking. At ten I told Buck, "When I get to be a man, I will never be carried home like that. It's embarrassing." He couldn't call our name until he sobered up.

As I matured, you would never find me out of my mental capacity to say yeah or nay, right or wrong. I've been around too many drunk people who were unable to help or defend themselves. What if someone came around and hit them on the head or robbed them? You mean to tell me throwing your guts up is worth that? I've never met a man who can land a convincing punch while drunk. All great athletes will tell you whiskey clouds your judgment. It throws you off balance and slows your reaction time. Quite frankly, it poisons your blood and makes you do things you might not ordinarily do.

There's tale of a woman notorious for beating on men got in a "he said she said" argument with a man known for speaking softly and carrying a big knife. Well, one thing led to another and the devil broke loose! The man went into a rage, pulled out a twelve-inch switch blade and cut both the woman's breasts off. It was a bad scene. She was rushed to the hospital where she stayed until she was well enough to recuperate at home.

In the same club years later, when I was a young adult, two childhood buddies of mine had too much to drink and argued over one of their sisters. Somebody saw what was about to go down and turned the lights on. I got in the middle of them to break up the argument and noticed both had their hands in their pockets. One bluffed, the other didn't. He pulled out a gun, the gun went off, and a bullet fired between my legs, straight into a young woman's calf.

No one screamed; they moved the party to the parking lot, including the two who instigated the ruckus. Commotions like this were common. There were no police or security guards, no bouncers, or doormen. Enter at your own risk and watch your back. Innocent bystanders beware. I rushed the woman to the hospital in my pink and gray Chevrolet where she was treated and released. She walks with a limp to this day.

It was unusually cold for a November afternoon in South Florida. A group of us tried to stay warm by playing ball. A nearby group of men warmed their hands over an open fire, drinking wine and wild turkey. My buddy took the ball, threw it up and down the dirt road, kicking dust around just acting the fool. He accidentally tossed the ball in the fire, setting off a chain reaction. The bottle knocked over, the wine spilt out, sparks flew up in a guy's face. He went into a maniacal frenzy, kicked the ball out the flames, and bashed Shelly across the back of the head with a two by four. My buddy was laid up for a while.

A few months before the cue ball incident, Daddy came home from a long day's work. It was Christmas eve and his boss had given him little nips as a Holiday bonus. Daddy had the bright idea to have me, his ten-year-old son, drink whiskey with him. "Danny boy is growing up; let's have a toast," he said. I should've been in bed waiting for Santa Clause to come through a hole in the tar paper, I'm gonna be a tough guy and join Daddy.

I swallowed one. Not too bad. Went down smooth. Poked out my chest out like a man. Sat for a few minutes, knocked back the second nip. My body swayed without permission.

"Danny. You all right?" Daddy waved his fingers in front of me back, forth, up, and down until I started to see double.

By then my stomach gurgled violently and Daddy had grown horns. Ran outside as fast as possible and threw up all over the lawn. Vomited two days straight. Mama, who had been in the kitchen cooking Christmas pies and rum cakes was mad as you know what. "Ought to leave you for giving my baby boy whiskey!" She and Daddy argued like drunken sailors for days straight. Spoiled the whole holiday.

Did Daddy get me drunk purposely? Was I on a path that he didn't want to see me go down? Remember now, my moral arc was shaped by my older brothers. At ten, I had already been exposed to things most adolescents don't dream about. Daddy knew of my hopes and desires, and I believe he knew a professional baseball career was imminent. Whether he did it knowingly or he had a momentary lapse in judgment, I thank him; seventy years later and I haven't drunk alcohol since.

Some of my closest friends smoke and drank. More than once I've had to carry a buddy over my shoulder and put them to bed passed out. While it never bothered me to be around them, it did strengthen my resolve to never drink. A man sloppy drunk is not a good look. You can buy a lot of things, but you can't buy time or a good reputation. A reputation is something you earn.

Take Me to the Water

MAMA AND DADDY POUNDED into our heads the importance of watching out for one another. Thou shalt always stick together: the eleventh commandment in our home, as important as honoring our father and mother. We might have fought like unneutered tom cats behind closed doors, but we put on a united front when we stepped outside. Calloway strong. Everyone knew if you messed with one of us, you messed with us all, no ifs, ands, or buts about it.

Stick together we did each week before the white throne of mercy. It was mandatory we go to Mount Olive's church school on the first and third Sunday. The second and fourth Sunday's we went to Hurst Chapel on Silver Beach Road.

Mama worked weekends when we were younger. Before she left the house, she dressed us in our Sunday best and prepared a breakfast of Cream of Wheat and orange juice. Daddy dropped us off on the church steps for the 9:00 class every other week. Kids sat impeccably dressed in one section, adults in another. Our bible teachers were untutored but profoundly intelligent. Like doting mothers, they always had open arms and listening ears. As the baby Calloway boy, the mothers showered me with extra care, and I basked in the attention.

Mount Olive was our second home: a small wooden building with no lights, no air, and a smoldering coal smudge pot to keep the mosquitoes away. The Reverend John Henry Dolphus presided over a congregation of few. In June 1930, he joined my parents in holy matrimony. "The groom and his bride have given themselves to each other by solemn vows, the joining of hands, the giving and receiving of rings. I pronounce that they are husband and wife, in the Name of the Father, and of the Son, and of the Holy Spirit." Reverend Dolphus remained head of the church until 1961 when Reverend Evans replaced him.

On the third Sunday every month we stayed for the Red Circle and the Baptist Young People's Union. Both organizations used the church for training dedicated to increasing Christian service in young people of the faith. The BYPU, in its training manual asks, "If West Point or Annapolis is necessary to the life of a nation, a training department of the church is vital to her life." Mount Olive was necessary to the life of the community.

The organizations met a critical need for the church's youth: socialization in a safe, respectable environment. Sure, we flirted with the girls and tussled with the boys, but it was clean fun. Late into the afternoon we'd fellowship over pound cakes, roasted peanuts, fresh-squeezed lemonade, and the best hand-cranked vanilla ice cream ever churned out. The church was our community center; a haven in the woods.

Mrs. Dolphus, the church mother, taught us everything. She took tens of children under her wing like a doting mother hen.

She didn't have children and cared for us as if we were her own. Right before service she rang a big, century-old cast iron bell, signaling the end of church school and the beginning of the 11:00 service.

The men filed into the sanctuary on the left, the women on the right. The middle was open to interpretation. No matter your location, every parent watched over every child; it mattered little to whom you belonged. The women's choir strutted in single-file singing "Climbing up the rough side of the mountain" with Mrs. Applewhite belting out the lead. It was beautiful. For a minute there, I daydreamed about directing the choir.

During summer revivals, every child not a member of the church had to sit on the front row, or what we called the mourners' bench. During these come to Jesus moments, the musty morning air hung heavier than the sinners' burdens. White clad church mothers, filled with the Holy Ghost, fanned cardboard cutouts, preached, prayed, and rebuked the devil.

"Get thee behind me Satan!"

In between supplications they'd spit snuff into tins concealed in their handkerchiefs. "Avoid the sea of fire and brimstone. Confess your sins today."

When Honeyman, Buck, and Faye joined the church mama was so happy. They were on their way to salvation. Four, five, six revivals passed with me still perched at the seat of mercy. Same white clad, snuff lipped church mothers whooped and hollered, and grabbed me by the head trying to drive the devil back to the scrubland.

"Satan, release this child." Spit. Wipe.

"Come to Jesus child." Wipe. Spit.

"Hallelujah!" Spit. Wipe.

Still didn't feel God talking directly to me like people say it happens. The only thing I felt was a giant mosquito sucking the blood from my ankle.

Everybody began to question, "What's wrong with that Calloway boy?"

Even Mama said, "Danny, it's time for you to give your life to the Lord."

Daddy said, "Leave the boy alone. He'll go when he's ready." In this regard, Daddy understood me.

I purposely didn't join the church during summer revival. An individualist, I am happiest and most confident when marching to the beat of my own drum. The only reason I didn't join the same time as everyone else was because I was a rebel. Half the time I didn't even know what I was resisting. Thank God for supportive parents who let me be me.

It was a third Sunday evening service when Reverend Dolphus said, "If anybody here is ready to join the church, to be baptized in Christ, to have an onward Christian experience, please come forward; the doors of the church are open."

Buck had already been a deacon for three years. Junior, Honeyman, Faye, and all my friends were on youth committees and in choirs. At fifteen, I heard the call and walked down the aisle, standing before the congregation like Jesus himself tapped me on the shoulder.

Filled with the Holy Ghost, everyone stood up and danced. Tambourines clanged, feet stomped, the pianist played that hand-clapping, toe-tapping music, "I turned it over to the Lord, He worked it out...Jesus can work it out..." It was another ten minutes or so before the clapping and shouting quieted. The pastor asked me to share why I was joining.

"The Calloway family is here," I said. "Been coming here my whole life. This is my church, so I want to become a member and do better by God."

On a Saturday two weeks later, I dressed in dungarees and a button up shirt and went to the ocean with five new members. The only beach open to Blacks was on Singer Island, then an untamed stretch of sand and dune. It provided ample fish and entertainment. Giant sea turtles deposited tennis-ball sized soft-shelled eggs in nests two-foot deep. For years, Granddaddy harvested the eggs. Considered aphrodisiacs, he sold dozens for hundreds of dollars. Today Florida law prohibits the sale or disturbance of the turtles.

When time came for my baptism the deacons wrapped my head in towels and, one on each side, lead me into four feet of water. Reverend Dolphus first said, "Baptism is a mechanism by which you publicly declare your faith. It is a sign you have already been saved but is not necessary for salvation." Before he lowered me in the water he said, "Repent and be baptized in the name of Christ Jesus for the remission of your sins." He held my nose and dunked me under three times.

"One for the Father." In that water.

"Two for the Son." In that water.

"Three for the Holy Ghost." In that water.

After the last dunk, I stood unmoved in the water expecting a feeling of something—anything. I felt wet and wanted to change my clothes. I didn't hear trumpets, no cherubim and seraphim hovered above me; no Holy, Holy, Holy. But if faith is the cornerstone, as Mama assured us, then I must trust in the Lord and go about my day.

Stepping out the water, I thought of something Mama told me years earlier: "Wherever you go take God with you." She was telling me God is a very present help in times of need and always with us. That if I live my life the way she and my father raised me I will be all right. Baptism doesn't save you; God's grace does.

Like my grandparents, parents, brothers, and sister, I was now a registered member of Mount Olive Missionary Baptist Church. The following day I began new members classes and established an irregular practice of reading the bible. I could feel it in my spirit: I still had a long way to go.

SCHOOL DAYS

Washington Junior High School

THE FIRST WEEK IN September Buck, our neighbor Claudia Bostick, and I walked five blocks hand in hand along a winding path through the woods, headed to a five-room structure known as Washington Junior High School. You know it today as Washington Elementary, but it started as a two-room shack in the woods. When Faye started two years later, she'd be in the middle of me and Buck skipping through the woods.

In the 1943 school, five rooms housed first through eighth grades. Each room had two grades. The ninth graders had their own. The school had no heat, electricity, or indoor plumbing. Kerosene stoves heated each room; one wood stove was rarely used. There was no janitor; ninth graders cut the wood for the stove, cleaned the kerosene lamps, swept the pine floors.

Just like home, the toilet was a batten outhouse surrounded by confederate jasmine and carpetweed. Latch the door good; always snoop before you poop. A bucket of wood ash and lime hung next to toilet paper in a bag. We were supposed to sprinkle a ladleful of lime into the devil's mouth to kill the stench and creepy crawlies. I don't think anyone did so. At the beginning and end of the school year neighborhood volunteers inspected the outhouse for rotted boards and critters, cleaned the pit and buried the waste in the woods. Life was good.

Grades one through twelve I went only to segregated schools. Didn't share the halls of academia with a single white person but I learned from their discarded books. Every teacher, whether you liked them or not, were second parents. If you misbehaved, they disciplined you. If you were hungry, they fed you. We had so many surrogate parents sometimes we forgot where we lived. Back then, it really was a village that raised you.

Ineria Hudnell was one of many women who stood in the gap. A prolific educator, thousands of children passed through her classrooms during her lengthy career. English and Art became popular subjects under her tutelage. In her classes we felt important, like everybody was somebody. Mrs. Hudnell was a small woman, but her percussive voice bounced off the shiplap and commanded respect. "Child hold your chin up. Always look a person in the eye. Take a deep breath and relax. Speak calmly and clearly. Let the mind release the information you want to share."

Her advice stayed with me long after my professional careers. I communicated better, spoke more confidently before crowds, and always stood tall. It took me a few years before I used words to get my point across. Until then, I used my fists.

As was my custom, I messed with the girls when Mrs. Hudnell's attention was elsewhere. One day Buck's classmate rushed through the door hollering, "Danny, Jimmie is beating up Buck!"

Without hesitation, I jumped up and ran to my big brother's defense. Mind you Buck, in the seventh grade, was older, larger, and brainier than me. But he was a mild-mannered mama's boy. Didn't play sports and barely worked the garden. He watched over me like a hawk; cared for Faye like a concerned parent. It's common for the youngest in the family to be spoiled and less motivated, and Faye fit the bill in earnest. And Buck was right there caring for her. He made sure her bows stayed in place, her clothes were pressed, that she had her bowl of Cheerios and milk. He taught me how to tie my shoes, ride a bike, drive a car. When I learned to care more deeply, it was because of him. Unlike me, he never balled his fist in anger or self-defense.

"Hey man," I said. "Leave my brother be."

"Little man, what you gonna do?" Jimmie asked me as he smacked Bernard in the head.

Hell may well freeze over before I'd let a challenge go unopposed. Fists tucked nose high, I threw a right hook to Jimmie's jaw like a young Joe Louis defending his title against Jersey Joe Walcott. Next, I unleashed a series of swift uppercuts to his chin and a left jab to the mouth. Jimmie, three years my senior and a half foot taller, admitted defeat.

"Hey man," he said, pulling away from my thrashing arms. "I ain't got no beef with you."

"If you got a problem with Buck, you got a problem with me," I said.

By now the hall was lined with girls on one side giggling and gasping and boys on the other side grinning in awe. Buck whispered, "Thank you little brother." Jimmie walked away hiding a busted lip under his hand; I strutted down the hall in victory, having earned the moniker "That Calloway boy," a worthy opponent ready to go the distance, on or off the field.

Never did I think I'd be the one supporting the underdog. At home Gene and Honeyman knocked me around so much I had to learn to protect myself. One day Mama saw them provoking me to tears. She grabbed me by the arm and said, "Danny, don't you ever let nobody push you around!" Mama didn't have to tell me anything twice. I never questioned a word out of her mouth, especially if it involved athleticism or ego. When Mama spoke, it was if God himself was talking to me.

Not all fights are fair, but victory is always sweet. Losing felt unnatural; I needed to win. It didn't matter whether the odds were stacked against me. As I matured, competition meant less about bravado and more about harnessing the intensity of rivalry without limiting my adversary's potential. A hard-fought win is sweeter when you know your opponent gave it his or her all. Helping Buck that day felt good. It demonstrated to me that I was able to help people in a losing position. I've been defending the weak and voiceless from that day forward.

Mrs. Hudnell wasn't too impressed. "See you after class," she said. "And your parents will be notified."

Known later in life as an authority on the area's Black history, Mrs. Hudnell was a stalwart in the community. She neither gave up on or looked down on us. Mrs. Hudnell, Mrs. Moore, and Mr. McDonald, my high school teacher and mentor, were amazing teachers. I haven't been in school for many years, but outside of my family, their influence on me was greatest.

Mama and Daddy would never fault me sticking up for my brother. Sure, Mama especially preferred that we use brain over brawn, but we did what we must. Young and overly audacious, fighting was in my blood. But I never used a knife or gun; and I wasn't a bully. My harmless taunting to some might appear otherwise, but when I was a child I spoke, understood, and thought as a child. I had yet to become a man. I defended myself and others using fists and fury. I hadn't yet learned how Muhammad Ali outsmarted his rivals by using the power of wit and words to get into his opponents' heads first before he knocked them out!

Buck was a gentle soul who used his heart and mind before his ego and fists. He was always the bigger man. He would have eventually gotten himself out of a tight bind. But he was Buck. Before I could read *Fun with Dick and Jane,* he was teaching me to read the Bible. Together we studied all my subjects, especially spelling, which I loved. I was in my element with anything that challenged me.

Promoted to Mrs. Harriette Moore's fifth and sixth grade class, I qualified for the spelling bee with five other students. "Your stellar performance has allowed you to compete in the trials. Whoever wins the competition may choose their team."

Always a competitor, I correctly spelled the words. For my team I chose two weak spellers who later became good buddies. As early as ten years old I championed for the underdog. I decided long ago to never be the obstacle that keeps someone else from reaching his or her full potential. If I can help them, I thought, then that's what I'm going to do. I've since built my life around that principle. My job is to help you understand you can make a difference with a modicum of ability.

We won convincingly, proving there are opportunities to lift or be lifted, to be a champion or be the one to champion.

I was crowned spelling bee champ and competed in the state championship. I made it far into the competition before I incorrectly spelled S-U-R-R-E-N-D-E-R. I hadn't considered the irony in that until recently. Here I am, a person who never gives in and yet I lose on the word surrender. Listen at the sound, visualize, sound it out.

Mrs. Moore was one of my favorite teachers. Don't know if it was because she was older, but she reminded me of someone's big mama: an ample bosomed gentle spirit. Whether it was talent or tenacity, she recognized something in me that led to my placement on the basketball roster alongside seventh, eight, and ninth graders.

I was so excited I could hardly contain myself. I played with the big boys on the sandlot. They knew of my talents and abilities and were happy to have me on the team. We practiced in vain on a floor of sawdust and gravel. When Principal Sinclair learned I was only in the fifth grade she and the coach pulled me off the team.

"I'm sorry Danny. Fifth and sixth grade students are not allowed on the team," she said. "If we make an exception for you, we must make an exception for others."

That didn't go over well with Frank Williams, captain of the Hawks. He said, "Well, none of us are gonna play." The team left the room refusing to participate in the next game. In no time I was back on the team.

Number 27-point guard, mouthy and brash like Muhammad Ali and unapologetically smug. Like Ali, I spoke up even when it was unpopular to do so. He was confident in his abilities and never dimmed his own light. There were plenty of people lined up to do that. I was an outstanding athlete and I too refused to dim my light. Ever. Even in the face of defeat, you will find me fighting until the buzzer.

The other fifth and sixth graders complained for days. In true form and fashion, I rubbed it in. "Y'all ain't good as me. Sit your rear ends down."

After a few days of practice, we stepped confidently into the West Palm Beach gym greeted by lights and a gym full of jeers. "Look at those wood boys. They can't play." Well, those city boys wiped the floor with us. They beat us 122 to 18. The fans booed us out the gym.

I cried for a week. Mama got so mad at me for brooding she threatened to pull me off the team. "If you can't lose like you win, don't play."

I've won many games over my career. I've cried over a few hard losses, too. As usual, Mama was right. I had to get to that place where I realized a hard-fought loss is as sweet a win. When you know you've done everything in your power, left every bit of you on the court, you learn, even through tears, sometimes you simply get outplayed.

Mama bought me a basketball. Daddy put up a hoop ten feet above ground on the coconut tree. The driveway, a mixture of shell rock and dirt, proved good enough a court as any. I dribbled, threw foul shots, and sunk two-and-three pointers until dusk every night. No net, no chain, pure. Faye retrieved loose balls until she had to go in the house.

I wonder if Mrs. Moore ever knew how her vote of confidence altered my life? That one devasting loss changed the trajectory of my life. Because of her faith in me, I was determined to do well in class. She used me as an example for future student-athletes, that one could play with older boys and excel scholastically.

When I reflect on my life and think of the people who had an influence on me, I put Mrs. Moore in that respected group. Some lessons are tough. Others are far-reaching in their simplicity, like the one she taught me on a warm Fall day after the game loss. She took my hands and noticed how dirty and unmanicured my nails were.

"Son, you might be a jock, but no girl will ever want to hold your hands looking the way they look. Wash your hands and scrub under your nails."

I never paid much attention to my hands other than keeping them free from injury. I'm an athlete. When not in school, I'm playing ball somewhere. Usually outdoors. Mama cut my nails once a month. The extent of my skin care routine consisted of Vaseline and Jergens lotion.

Mrs. Moore was a respected teacher who watched over her students like a mother bear protects her cubs; I had no reason to doubt her. As soon as I got home, I brushed and scrubbed under my nails until clean. Mrs. Moore might have saved me years of embarrassment.

She also told me smoking would stunt my growth. No need to place too much muster in that because I wasn't a smoker. What's more, in the early twentieth century cigarettes weren't advertised as bad for your health. It was an accepted norm; glamourous, albeit misleading. Advertisements even showed doctors smoking their favorite brands. If nothing else, you looked like a big man with a Chesterfield hanging from your mouth.

But anything that even hinted at messing with my athleticism had to have at least some truth, right?

I had always wondered what the allure was in smoking, whether cigars, pipes, or the Marlboros perched between cowboy's lips. We rolled Daddy's cigarettes, but he dared us to ever smoke them. The sticks couldn't be too loose or too tight. We had to find the perfect amount of tobacco to use. Like the tale of Goldilocks, it had to be exactly right. Deliberately, Gene and Honeyman rolled the Bugle tobacco through the machine too tightly. They figured out a way to keep the rejects without Daddy finding out. One day they were dragging on a square. Everyone in the family knew I was tattletale. To keep me quiet, they gave me the duck.

"Here man," Gene said. "Take a drag."

"Yeah man, it'll make you big and strong," said Honeyman.

He was pulling my leg, I know. But I had to see for myself what all the fuss was about. Never have I blindly followed behind someone nor gone along just to get along. No, I think for myself; it makes for better company. Anyhow, I put the inch-long piece up to my mouth, took a drag, and singed my lip. That's all it took.

"Take this thing," I told Gene.

"Stop being a sissy," Honeyman said.

Well, if it burns, it's bad. Plus, I had too much ego to allow anything to mess with my good looks. How could I stare my girl in the eyes with a nasty sore on my lip? Never again has a cigarette touched this mouth. Fool me once, shame on you; fool me twice, watch out!

My decision to not smoke or drink had nothing to do with Mama and Daddy, though I've always wanted to make them proud. It was because I don't like anything that leaves a bad taste in my mouth.

See, a person who goes along to get along never gets far. March to your own beat. You'll like yourself better. That may not be the best thing for a lot of people; but it worked for me. Now, I'll allow you to do the same. If you want to walk at your own pace, so be it. But if you are under my auspices, you are going to do it my way until you can show me something different. If you can prove your way is superior, I'll change. Those were two of her final lessons, but they have stayed with me forever. To this day, I think of her every time I wash my hands. I wish I had told her thank you.

In 1951 a Christmas day bombing in Mims, Florida took the life of Mr. Harry Moore. Nine days later his lovely wife, and one of my favorite teachers, Mrs. Harriette Moore, died from injuries sustained in the explosion. They had just celebrated their 25th wedding anniversary.

Mr. Moore started the Brevard County chapter of the NAACP in 1934 and actively took part in the civil rights movement. He spoke out against racial inequalities and the mistreatment of Blacks. His activism made him a prime target of the Ku Klux Klan. In 2008 the FBI reviewed earlier investigations, but probable suspects died before any arrest were made. The case was closed.

It's hard to make sense of incidents like the Florida bombing or any number of school-related tragedies that have plagued our nation over the last twenty-five years. Like the algebra Mrs. Moore taught, some problems are hard to solve. If you're lucky, you figure it out. Or you don't. Then grace appears in a smile, a moonlit night, a tender embrace that reminds us good still exists in the world. We walk our paths and hope our living is not in vain.

Palmview Junior High School

PALMVIEW JUNIOR HIGH IN West Palm Beach was my second home from September 1950 through May 1952. The brick building had a gym and an outdoor basketball court. Everything Washington lacked, Palmview had, including heat, electricity, inside plumbing. It was the first time I read in the glow of a fluorescent light or peed into a toilet that flushed. But we still learned from used books.

We caught the bus in one of two locations: the east side near Old Dixie or the west in front of Washington Junior High, which was now Washington Elementary, no longer home to the upper grades. Buck and I raced the sunrise to catch the 6:30 a.m. bus.

Students from Jupiter sat sleepily within the death trap on wobbly wheels. The bus driver, Mr. John Webb, always greeted us by name. "Fine morning Danny." "Good to see you Bernard." He performed his job with pride. No one cut up. If the bus driver said, "Y'all sit down and shut up," we'd sit down and shut up. No backtalk, no disrespect.

Two or three girls saved seats for me, hoping I'd squeeze in beside them. "Danny, sit with me." "No Danny; come over here." They'd each vie for my attention. I preferred to sit with

Delores Webster, my heartthrob since birth, but she boarded at the next stop. By then I had already been seated.

Soon, I lost interest in Riviera Beach girls, including Delores. I grew bored with the familiar. I wanted to see what the West Palm Beach girls had to offer. In my eyes, they were the forbidden fruit that I had to taste.

When the bus rolled up to Palmview, forty kids in tow, a crowd hung in front. We didn't know if they were coming for us or waiting for the school bell to ring. Everyone on the bus got scared when they saw kids yelling, holding sticks and stones. No one wanted to get off.

As soon as Mr. Webb unfolded the doors I walked out. No one followed behind me, so I turned back and yelled, "Y'all get off this bus. Nobody gonna bother you." The crowd quieted. I held out my hand stiff long, like Moses parted the Red Sea, and the people moved aside. We marched between them into the school without care or concern.

Coincidentally, two of the bullies became my close friends, proving that you can work through differences when you get to know someone. Clark Martin, the main instigator, used to take me to his house after school for bologna sandwiches and mangoes after he got to know me. He lived in West Palm Beach two blocks from the school, so I'd wait there for the second session bus. We stayed close friends until he died in 2015.

My homeroom teacher Mrs. Brown was reared in Riviera Beach and knew Mama and her sisters. Something on my mind, she listened. Forgot my meal ticket, no problem. She was one of many mothers.

Washington didn't have a cafeteria; we ate in the classroom. Buck made a lunch of fried chicken, or a fish sandwich, no mustard, heavy on the mayonnaise. Mama packed me an apple every day. I drank two pints of milk for strong bones. I took a two-hour nap after school. These things Mama insisted I do to become who I had envisioned.

At Palmview, a dietician passed out lunch. You could buy a meal ticket for eighty cents. That bought you a week's worth of ham and cheese sandwiches, milk, and a donut. One dollar got you a lunch plus an extra milk and donut. Nowadays, you can't buy spit for a dollar much less a week's worth of lunches.

That first day at Palmview I met one of my closest friends. Sellaway didn't know me when I got on the bus that day, but he knew me when I got off. He was the big boy of the group, a few inches taller and a year older. We played basketball before and after school on the outdoor court; there wasn't one in Riviera. That's why the West Palm Beach boys were so good. They had a place to practice.

They weren't good in every way. In fact, some things they did defied convention. Faye and Buck were the smartest, and I made decent grades. Some of my friends used to peek at my paper during exams. During one test, an unmotivated classmate copied everything off my paper including my name. Just think about it; he had to be pretty dumb to copy my name. If you're gonna cheat, at least be smart about it.

Start of the school year, all the boys signed up to play basketball. Coach Bruce read off the list and said, "Calloway, you and Lester transfer students?"

"Yes sir, we are."

"You boys can't play; no activity bus. I can't be responsible for getting you home."

He wouldn't let us try out. We were so disappointed. But Mama taught us that nothing is ever so bad that you can't get over it. "Weeping may endure for a night, but joy cometh in the morning." She was always right; another lemonade moment.

After the season, intramurals started. Doc and Sellaway were in class 7A. I'm in 7B with Lawson. And the best team came out of 7C. 7D was just okay. The whole school came to the gym to see what I, a wood boy, could do. "That boy can't play ball," they said. "They don't even have a hoop in the country."

We won the tournament. I was leading scorer and got MVP. That was my coming out party. It felt good as drinking a cold jar of lemonade under the mango tree. A few years later, when I played for Roosevelt High School, Coach Bruce refereed one of my games. By now, I was All-American and had set school records. Fortune favors the bold.

He said, "Calloway, I need to tell you something."

"What's that Coach?"

"The worse mistake I ever made—and I hope you can forgive me—was not letting you play for me in 1950."

"Aww coach, I been forgot that," I said. I hadn't really forgotten about. That snub stayed a sore spot with me for a long time. I still held it against him, but I wouldn't let him know that. He thought he was doing the best thing, but it hurt me to the core. I held that over Coach Bruce's head until he died.

I played Varsity baseball in ninth grade and never missed an inning. Second year, three days before the opening day game in Pompano a big fight occurred, and the pitcher and star player got thrown off the team. Coach Brooks said, "What are we going to do with no pitcher? I guess I'll have to play Freeman." Freeman, at 6'8" was an outstanding basketball player but not a good pitcher.

"Coach, I can pitch."

"You can pitch Danny?" he asked.

"Best pitcher in town, sir," I said confidently. "I'll practice a couple days and show you."

He was convinced the first day. I pitched, struck out ten, and the game ended in a tie. I felt good about my performance. Coach Brooks was pleased with his decision. But the happiest person was Sellaway. When we got home, he told anybody who would listen. He didn't play Little League ball, so he had never seen me pitch. But I bet he remembers that day.

The Five Fs

Middle School is a challenging age for children and a trying time for teachers and parents. It is critical for us to be more active in the schools and their communities because as my stories have shown, it takes a village to raise a child. Let's strengthen the village. When I was in school many years ago, all of our teachers stood in the gap. It was expected. I challenge you the reader, young and mature, to volunteer in your local schools.

The administrator with a middle school in Riviera contacted me to help make a difference with her students who were displaying bad, unruly behavior and put an end to what has been happening at schools around the county. Children don't want to learn anymore. There is something wrong when there is a black school with two thirds white teachers who don't want to be there.

Last time I spoke to the private school it was time for them to give back. They have no idea what is going on in some of the schools or communities. The kids in private or charter schools are worrying about what to wear, not the repercussions suffered as a result of breaking the code: if you snitch, you gonna end up in a ditch, you gonna have some stitch.

But I say, if you see something say something. Those people who wonder if they should do something, should do something. When I was in school the louder they barked the shallower the wound. I was mouthy; so, when they had a chance, they took it. Trouble is, I'm not easily scared so codes are for my locker.

Bordering S Avenue, Monroe heights was integrated late 1970s from what was once all white, remnants of the wall that separated us still standing. Their exodus from the area we called the great white flight.

Community, to be effective, needs both black and white, male, female team concept. Take the challenge and effect change. Everybody wants to be free to learn something, but I will not give you a freebie. We need you parents, we need you teachers, we need you to show up when you show up. Who is the person doing the heavy lifting in the community and making a difference? Find them. Emulate her or him. Do what you can in your schools and communities to stand in for those who can't stand for themselves. Ask your school administrator about the Five Fs and how you can help in the classrooms.

The reason why kids fuss and cuss in front of their parents and teachers is they don't have respect for them. When we have the parents get involved with the kids at home and at school it's a beginning. That's why we put together the different programs that are available for you too. The "friends of the school" are volunteers and committee members the organizers bring to and coordinate in your middle school. Let's start regaining trust with our children today using food and fun as the great equalizer that brings everyone together.

Roosevelt High School

THE ROOSEVELT HIGH SCHOOL sociology class intrigued me, not because of the subject but because of the learned, articulate teacher who knew how to engage his audience. A natural orator, Mr. S. Bruce McDonald cut through you with words. He stands tall among giants and continues to fight the good fight. In my eyes he is the eighth wonder of the world.

How fortunate was I in 1953 to be in the first class he taught after his discharge from the army? Since the year we met, he has taught me more than any teacher I've ever known. Mr. McDonald instilled in many men an unrivaled since of self-worth. He has been a great mentor to me for over sixty-five years. I have him to thank for much of the humanitarian work I have done over the years.

Sitting in the front row of class my junior year, I drunk in every single word he spoke. He taught us to set our sails for horizons outside of Riviera Beach.

"Palm Beach County is not the end all," he'd say. "There's a big world out there and it's yours for the taking." Walking back and forth as he lectured, I was struck by his confidence and style. He wore high-waisted polyester blend slacks with sport coat and button-down shirt that accentuated his stout body. He always encouraged. "The Earth is expansive. Get out and see it. Don't box yourself in."

Articulate to the nth degree, he could talk with everyone. I've not known a person who he hasn't positively influenced. At his ninetieth birthday celebration I had the honor of sharing with his guests something he told me in eleventh-grade that had a profound impact on me: "Loosen the reins while you are in high school. Play the field a little. Don't get bogged down," he'd tell us. "When you become an adult, you'll better understand different personalities and which one's best suit you."

Mr. McDonald commanded attention like E. F. Hutton; when he spoke, everybody listened. I took him at his word and stopped going out with one girl but started dating damn near every girl in school. I'm quite sure that's not what he meant when he told us to play the field a little and expand our horizon.

The horizon stretches everywhere; over hills, valleys, and distant shores. Even with an iron clad life blueprint, some things are going to remain out of your control. My horizon had a pitcher's mound and white rubber slab.

Mr. Brooks was my physical education teacher and baseball coach. He taught the fundamentals of sport to every student athlete who passed through the halls. I never missed an inning.

He taught me how to throw, shoot, hit. In 1953 I started as a second hitter behind Richard Mitchell. Four years I never missed an inning or sat or the bench. Beside my family and friends, Mr. Brooks was my biggest supporter.

When I was inducted into the 2004 Roosevelt High School Sports Hall of Fame and voted the greatest athlete to come out of the school, the best baseball player ever, Mr. Brooks was there. Riviera Sports Hall of Fame voted me the best athlete out of Riviera; Mr. Brooks was there. When the Pirates signed me, he was at the house sitting beside Mama and Daddy, asking lots of questions.

I wore the number 21 in baseball, based on a centerfielder from the Cleveland Indians named Bob Lemon. He won twenty games every year. He used to be a third baseman. But he was also a good pitcher. I was going to be one of the exceptional pitchers. I had control, the curve ball, the fast ball, the changeup.

I always thought I had the advantage if I threw hard or slow, leaving the batter off-balance as he tried to guess what I planned to throw. I don't change stance. I throw the ball with the same motion. The magic is in the grip.

Roosevelt High had the first modern gym in the area. Lights, scoreboard, urethane floor. Twelve hundred students from Jupiter, Riviera, and West Palm housed under the same roof. Fans shouted, "Break the Clock!" Sixteen out of twenty-seven we broke the clock, which means we scored one hundred or more points. We were hard to beat.

I made all American in basketball. Point guard and point forward, I averaged triple doubles before anyone knew what that was. I was third on the team to score 13.2; led the team in rebounds 16.3; assists, 15.4. I was the Oscar Robinson of Roosevelt High. However, you don't spell team with an "I." What I was able to accomplish was with the help of my teammates. Remember this: Success in life is in direct correlation to how well you work with others.

Pat Quince was a year behind me but one of the best basketball players to grace the team. We were the Magic Johnson and Kareem Abdul-Jabbar duo of our time. And it wasn't always pretty. We both had a lot of bravado. One day he and I were playing river ball during PE class on one end of the gym, showing off for the pretty girls at class on the other end. Before I knew it, horseplay went left, and Pat strong-armed me. He was a lean two hundred ten pounds to my muscular one hundred sixty. At six feet six inches tall, he had five inches on me too. Well, he shoved me and knocked me off balance. In return, I charged and slammed him against the wall. He raised me off the floor with one arm like Mighty Joe Young lifted Primo Carnera off the stage on his show's opening night. His hand, clenched firmly around my neck, held me dangling mid-air like a rag doll. He was about to wipe up the floor with me.

He outweighed me, but he couldn't outwill me. I summoned everything I had to reach out arm's length to push his head back. Someone had alerted Faye, who by then was in the boy's locker room looking for a weapon. Before I knew it, she was banging a 12 oz. glass Coke bottle across his arm yelling, "Put my brother down!" Here I am a six-foot one-inch jock trying to save face before the ladies and my little sister comes to my rescue. I was never more embarrassed, but we continued to dominate on the court.

I took care of Faye; she wasn't supposed to take care of me. It all started when I failed to watch over her when Mama was away from home. Bernard had gone to the five and dime for candy. Playing marbles with neighborhood boys I took my attention off Faye, who had wandered to a shady spot near a patch of fountain grass to make mud cakes and pies.

When Mama came home and saw her baby girl sitting shirtless in the middle of a nasty puddle in an area where snakes hide out, she nearly lost the good sense for which she's known. Faye, happy as cereal in milk, sat unfazed. Mama snatched her up and placed her on the porch. She came for me and tore my skinny legs up! Thank God a coral or gator didn't slither out the grass near Faye. Been watching over little sister ever since.

Faye was introverted. She sat timidly on the bus in the mornings, kept to herself most hours in class. Like Buck, Faye was God fearing. Not the social butterfly, but my little sister all the same. I can't imagine a time in my life without her.

There was a young man in her class that liked her. Faye hadn't dated yet. She was either too shy or thought I'd beat up her suitors. One Sunday evening the boy that likes her comes by the house toting a friend. "What are you boys doing here," I asked.

"Rock, we came to talk to Faye."

"Does Faye know you coming by to talk to her?"

"No. We just want to talk to her."

"But why…" I stepped off the porch and onto the sidewalk. Before they finished their sentence, I said, "Listen to me well and don't ever forget what I'm about to tell you. There is no good reason for you to ever call or come by this house again for my sister."

I kept boys from talking to Faye. They know I have to okay it before they call her. They didn't have to talk to Mama and Daddy, they had to talk to me. I was the police before I became the police. When the pressure is on, I am at my best.

Records set and broken by me for three years might have had something to do with my number 17, which in the bible signifies "complete victory." Or it could have been the superstition I had that forbid Mama from washing my game socks. She could wash them at the end of the season only, when I'd pack them away for the next year. Those socks could have walked away on their own they smelled so badly. The socks may have kept me on a winning streak, but I had to keep my Chuck Taylor's to air on the porch.

During a basketball game in my senior year I caught an elbow to the mouth and lost a front tooth. Never lost a minute of play. The coach called time, sealed the socket, and put me back on the floor. We won the game in true form.

We were the best-uniformed team in the state, clean, neat, and groomed. Every three weeks we got our hair cut into a low English by the neighborhood barber, Mr. John Henry Shellman, who we called Man Sherman because that's how he pronounced his name.

His shop was his home's enclosed front porch: One barber's chair and a few double slat back wooden folding chairs to sit on while waiting your turn. He was the only barber on the north end. It took him two hours to cut one head with hand clippers and a razor. Honeyman, Buck, and I were there so long we'd carry our lunch with us. If a car passed, he'd stop cutting to see who was driving. Our friends walked by and teased us. "Loose that man, loose that man. Let him go!" Mr. Shellman was never in a hurry. Years later he built a shop. Generations have walked through his doors.

Our team travelled throughout the state of Florida, going as far north as Jacksonville, and south to Key West. The best team we played was from Carver High in Miami. If we happened to win, the home team fans threw eggs at our bus. It was the same when we played Booker T. Washington, North Western, Dillard, Daytona, teams in Jacksonville, or Delray. It was not unusual for us to travel 10 hours round trip by bus, unable to eat until we slumped sleepy-eyed and hungry into our host house. Overall, it was an exciting time. I wouldn't trade it for stock.

I set many records for Roosevelt High's Maroon Devils, but none more noteworthy than an ERA of 0.67. For perspective, the lowest recorded single-season earned run average in National League history was 0.86, posted in 1880 by Tim Keefe after 105 innings. I pitched in every game we played with a 37.1 record.

As my star rose, I was compared to an older Negro League player named Eddie Macon. Although contributions to the sport are many, the face of black baseball is seen only in a few. Many of the League's most talented players entered the sunsets of their lives unknown or forgotten. As a tribute to him, I became the Little Shamrock. We played together a few years later on the Riviera Tigers. I had never met Mr. Macon before the Tigers, yet he bragged to everyone that he taught me how to pitch.

In Irish folklore, the shamrock's status as a symbol of luck go back to the Druids believing that carrying a three-leaf clover allowed them to see spirits and ward off danger. On the other hand, a four-leaf clover offered them magical protection. I read about "the Fighting Irish" in the Sunday paper and learned everything I could about them. The fact that they fought was good enough for me. Eventually, my nickname evolved to "The Rock." I was tough, fearless, and willing to fight to defend my honor, family, and justice.

Buck used to say, "Man, that's gonna get you in a lot of trouble. If a man got a gun, you ain't even gonna run. You gonna figure out how to wrestle him to the ground."

I've been accused of being cocky many times. No bullets, no bite. Everybody feels nerves at times, but once the game starts you've got to find a way to calm down. The iron-willed do well under pressure.

The day of an important game against Fort Lauderdale's Dillard High School, the dean announced over the intercom: "Attention students. Make sure you show up later today to cheer on the Maroon Devils and their pitcher, Dan Shamrock Calloway. He's sure to bring the heat."

Classmates, teachers, and parents came to see us win and we delivered. When they announced the lineup, the crowd was fever pitch. "And now, introducing your starting lineup: Jones. Quince. Lowry. Lawson, and the little Shamrock!" Struck out the first at bat. As the game neared the final inning, Coach Brooks said, "Shamrock, take us home."

You could hear people in the stands booing and mouthing me saying, "Look at that old man with the big flannel pants. He thinks he's Satchel Paige."

I never took kindly to lip. "You all can build a woodpile with those bats," I'd say. "You can't do nothing with this." I'd dare them to mouth a word. Then the next batter goes down for the count. Won the game 10-2.

In the streets, football season ran from October to January. September was still too hot, though you might find us playing pudding back. No tops, no shoulder pads, no helmets; just killing each other for sport. We played among unmarked graves on white sand north of the cemetery. I was the smallest, at times the youngest, always the boldest. Wherever my brothers went, I went. Whatever my brothers did, I eventually did better.

Playing one day somebody threw a block on my blind-side, my leg buckled, and a grapefruit-sized knot exploded from my knee. I went to the hospital where they diagnosed me with a kneecap injury which required surgery, broken pieces of patella put together with pins. I thought my professional baseball career had ended where the nameless lay buried in peace.

Mr. Brooks told the football coach I should be quarterback and by the time the season got underway, I was a standout wide receiver, out-running and out-maneuvering the best. Fast as Speedy Gonzales, I ran the football down with precision and style, catching balls sky-high, thick air, one hand over shoulder mid-flight. Odell Beckham had nothing on me. In 1953 the Pittsburg Courier listed me as one of the top twenty high school athletes in the country. Can't touch this.

Still, Daddy never wanted me to play football. He thought I would get hurt and ruin my chances of being signed. Just a few weeks earlier scouts with the Chicago Cubs came by the house to speak with Mama and Daddy about a contract.

"Sir. We'd like your son to join Banks and Baker in our Farm Club in Des Moines."

"He can't play," Mama interrupted. "Danny's got another year in school. I won't let him leave school to go play baseball."

"School?" they asked in disbelief. "We saw him playing with the men."

"Well that's nothing new; he's been playing with men since eighth grade." Mama was firm. "Talk to us next year."

Anyhow, I proved Daddy's greatest fear come true when I broke my ankle during the first game of the season. I completed a few plays on an injured ankle. The pressure was on. We could finish them off. Eventually coach pulled me. Daddy cried like a baby.

If you were to ask me what the common denominator was that bridged the three sports I played in school, it would be the ability to withstand pressure. I was a clutch player. I pitched all the big games and hit three in the lineup. I took the winning shot with seconds on the clock. The more the pressure, the better I performed. I never let anything control me, including regret.

I got put out of my homeroom by Mrs. Holliday, a teacher who loved me like her son, because I did something regrettable to an unsuspecting classmate. If someone else had picked on this same girl, I'd be mad as a dog with rabies.

Girls gave Mrs. Holliday their prom escort's name to make sure none brought army men. Grace, whose chubby cheeks I pinched daily, was bigger than anyone in class, so heavy in fact that we called her Shotput. She hadn't given the teacher her escort's name yet, so showing-off I said, "I'll tell you what Shotput. I think I'm gonna take you to prom. Mrs. Holliday is waiting on me to give her my date's name too."

"Oh Daniel," she said. "I'm going to tell momma and my brother you are going to take me to prom." I think Grace was the only one who called me Daniel.

She blissfully told the teacher I was to be her escort. A week before the big day, Mrs. Holliday, before the entire class said, "Everyone has turned in their date's name except Daniel." She looked at me and asked, "Daniel, are you accompanying Grace? She said you were taking her."

I stood in my seat like a bad-mannered fool, turning toward Grace who smiled. "I am taking Shotput," I said, trying not to bust out laughing. "The only reason I haven't confirmed yet is because I am waiting to hear from the bus company. For me to take Shotput I need to carry her in a big bus."

The class erupted in laughter. Boys pointed at her jeeringly; girls covered their mouths in disgust. Grace cried unconsolably. Regrettably, an innocent prank on my part had spiraled out of control. Everyone knew I wasn't going to take Grace, but I never expected it to go this far left. I got caught in the moment. It's one thing to be a trickster, another thing to hurt someone for laughs.

God should have punished me for that. Grace should have never spoken to me again, but she forgave me. We became friends despite my inexcusable behavior. Never poke fun at someone else's expense.

Such is the call and response of life.

BIRDIES AND PARS

Montauk Downs Country Club

I HAD FOUR DAYS left to train when the Pirates cut me. No money, no job. My friends told me that were headed up north to caddy. Sellaway drove me and three other guys north, then went to his job in New Jersey. We paid fifteen dollars a week for a small room in a house surrounded by potato fields and ducks.

Every morning at sunrise, we walked five miles to the golf course, caddied thirty-six holes, walked five miles back. Sometimes we stopped at the diner for a breakfast of coffee, eggs, and grits. On our days off we showed off at

We caddied for wealthy club members at three links-style courses: Southampton, Shinnecock Hills, and National Golf Clubs; pristine sloping hills and meadowland perched between the Peconic Bay and Atlantic Ocean.

Ed Furgol, the 1954 U.S. Open champ, about to start a round, noticed my name on the Pirate's injured list in the Post. He asked his caddy, "Hey, isn't this the Dan Calloway who once caddied at the Seminole?"

"Yeah, that's him," they said. "He's not playing anymore. Hurt his shoulder in camp."

"Well how can I reach him? I could use him," Ed said.

"He's caddying off of Country Road 39," Daddy Cane offered.

A few weeks later, the same Ed Furgol, the club pro, offered me the caddy master position at picturesque Montauk Downs Country Club. I accepted the position and recruited sixteen men. We lived for free in barrack-style housing on a horse farm near the course. Every day the Manor hotel fed us a hearty, free meal.

It was easy to recruit when guys stood to make hundreds of dollars a week, with free room, and board. I kept many of the same caddies for the years. Sometimes I'd have my friends from home come up and work, though a few of them were already here. With my professional baseball career over, I came to realize that just maybe I was born to do something else. Caddying and instructing felt right, so much so that I continued to do it for fifty years. I came alive on the fairway, coaching members along. I felt like I was doing what I was supposed to do.

Me and the caddies spent good times hanging out at the College Inn. I dressed in shark skinned suits and stingy brimmed hats and sported a trimmed goatee. I was sweet poppa sweat, the women's pet; Dapper Dan, the ladies' man; Impy Dimp, the poor girl's pimp. Women remained my Achilles heel.

We traveled forty miles to the Bluebird Inn in Riverhead and dance to Sam Cook and Lloyd Price. Off on Mondays, Sunday evenings were spent in Spanish Harlem where we wined and dined some of the prettiest women in New York. Women were easy to come by and hard to resist. With a pocketful of game, a pretty face became a pawn to capture.

Sellaway taught me two things I didn't learn from anybody but him and I'll never forget what he said. He and I shared a room while living in Jamaica Queens. He was a gentleman in every sense of the word. A loyal friend, he stuck close like a brother. Every night I was in the clubs picking up women. I flattered them and told them, "Baby, you know I love you." I wasn't sincere; I just wanted to get in their pants. I'm not proud of that but I'm telling you my story.

A godly man from the time we met in seventh grade, Sellaway never smoked, drank, or cussed. He was gentle like Buck. I guess he thought I'd be damned to hell or something because having seen enough, he took me aside and said, "Man, let me tell you something. You don't have to tell all those women you love them."

"Well I got to get them," I said.

"Naw man, you gonna get them anyhow. There's something about you that attracts women. Stop doing all that!"

I had never seen myself in the way Sellaway described. Gene and Honeyman buttered up women, so I thought vainly that was the only way to get them. Never did I imagine there was another way or that I was playing with their feelings. I took Sellaway's advice and when I stopped fawning over them, they swarmed on me like honeybees.

"See. I told you," Sellaway said. "Love is a precious word. You should never tell anyone you love them when you don't."

Those words penetrated my soul. It's what took me so long to get married. I did not use that word again until I meant it.

"You should read the bible every day," he said. "Really you should read it before you go to bed and before you rise."

"Well let's just stick to before I go to bed," I told him.

Mama taught us to get on our knees and thank God every night, but I didn't start reading the Bible outside of church until I was an adult. I was washed in the blood of the lamb and baptized in the sea of my ancestors; but it was Joseph L. Sellaway who made me think about salvation.

Everyone wants to place blame for the things wrong in their lives. But I stand up for my frailties as well as my strengths. I was a playboy. This I admit without shame because I treated women with respect. How would I look mistreating any woman knowing that I must answer not only to God but to Faye and Mama? But I stand by my word. I told every woman with whom I was involved that I was not ready to settle down. Now, if they weren't ready to read the tea leaves, that is on them.

I won't run nor will I duck. That's why I never messed with married woman. When you are in the streets fumbling around with a woman who belongs to another man, eventually you've got to run and pay the piper. What if their man comes? I never had a man running after me and no man have, I ever run from.

I thank Sellaway for intervening when he did. His words caused me to reflect in ways that I had not done before. I won't say I became a saint after our conversation, but I did approach women differently.

Working in New York I was free to dream again; big, unselfish dreams. I earned enough to send money home to help Mama and Daddy. I dressed how I wanted, ate what I liked, reflected on life, and healed. Early evenings we smashed balls onto fairways lined by piney woodland and scrub; it felt like home.

Ed, the club pro, saw me drive a ball three-hundred feet down the center of the fairway, avoiding water to the left, bunkers on the right.

"Danny, you're rather good," he said. "How would you like to be my demonstrator?"

I thought a demonstrator was a person who walked up and down the street with a sign and bullhorn. Wrong. I soon became proficient at how to move it to the left, move it to the right, fade, and hook, keep it low, keep it high—basic fundamentals. Daddy's earnest lessons paled in comparison to Furgol's skillful instruction. He taught me that no matter what you know, to be great, continue to learn your craft. Before long, we held members' clinics.

"Danny, hit me a six-foot draw." His amplified voice rung from his megaphone, fifty eager students watching closely. That means I'll hit to the right and draw it back with a little curve to it right to left.

"Now hit me a Hogan fade." I hit it to the left and fade it six to eight feet back to the right.

"Hit the ball six feet off the ground." I'd hit it under the wind Texas style.

I didn't know it at the time, but those hundred people who watched me execute each stroke, paid one hundred dollars per person for the honor. After each one-hour clinic he gave me a crisp hundred-dollar bill. He paid me to show the club owners how to play high lob shots through sea spray misting in the air.

I was a natural golfer. When I look at a golf course, in my mind, I know I'm going to make at least four birdies. I hit the ball hard and long. On a par five I hit the ball at least two eighty. I know If I Rarely did a leave a par five without a birdie.

In 1959 I was a twenty-one-year-old man making forty-five dollars an hour teaching private lessons to movie stars and business tycoons. Some days I made more than two and three hundred dollars. Long before I earned my first dollar, I promised Mama I would take care of her one day. Twice monthly I sent home a generous check which helped pay Faye's tuition in full before Labor Day each year. Blessed, money was never an issue.

Caddies kept their cash in suitcases, sometimes thousands of dollars. I trained them to be their own bank and required they get postal money orders made out to themselves. We had that amount of money because we did a lot of gambling.

To pass the time, we often played dice and cards in the caddy pen. Four of us played a game called Pitty Pat at a table made of plywood atop a workbench, sitting on chairs of wooden soda crates. The object is to be the first player to get rid of all of your cards in your hand by matching your card with the top card in the pile. The player to the dealer's left goes first.

I spoke Spanish to let Clark know what card was needed. The other guys didn't know we were signaling to one another, so we got away with it for a while. If I needed an eight, I'd say ocho and if Clark had it, he'd throw the eight on the table. If Clark needed a queen, he'd say reina, and if I had a queen, I'd throw it on the table.

Well one day while me and Clark were winning all the money, Eddie Lee walks in laughing. The guys we were playing said, "Man, you jitterbugs is lucky." Eddie said, "them fools ain't lucky, they are speaking Spanish."

Johnny said, "Hey fools. Give us back our money."

Clark grabbed his money. I grabbed mine and turned the table over. We fought on top of crates like we were in a shootout at the O.K. Corral. Our backs to the wall, we had to think fast before pandemonium broke loose. We threw those boxes around like mad men until we had a chance to run for the car, never to play together with those men again.

Ninety percent of caddies in early to midcentury America were Black. Some were old enough to be your daddy. Many were dropouts, drunks, or ex-cons. Most worked because they made more money in a day than they'd make in a week. However, if it rained, we made no money. We didn't have insurance, paid time off, or a pension.

Once perceived as a menial job, caddying has become a high-paying vocation to which many ambitious men and women are attracted. Years ago, Black caddies were a requirement at elite clubs. Today, there are few if any Black caddies in the PGA.

White or Black, a good caddy will carry a towel in hand, one end wet to wipe down the balls. Good caddies also know that the neater they dress, the better groomed they are, the more business they get. When I became caddy master, the first thing I outlawed were the drunks. No sleeping in your clothes smelling like an open bottle of bad whiskey. I've fired many caddies for being out all night sloppy drunk coming on the course looking like they've been rolling around in a pigsty.

I made a rule when I became caddy master. If you have a problem, come to me. That is what I told my caddies. Then I told my boss if he or any of the members have a problem with any of my caddies, see me. I didn't want any member saying they were firing my men. You hired me to be responsible for the caddies. I subcontract them out to the course. I will handle them. That is how I ran things.

Well, one of my caddies had a problem. He wanted to get out, but I didn't have anyone to put him with, so he got belligerent. I walked from my desk and away from the pro shop so no one would hear us. I told him, "Let me tell you two things you need to remember. Not only do I have authority to fire you and hire you. Number two, I'm a deputy sheriff. I can arrest you anytime you even think you're going to put your hands on a law enforcement officer. But I can forget all that. We can go in these here woods and I can tear your head off."

This man was from New York and thought he could do what he had done with a few other caddy masters and threaten me. I said, "Nobody threatens me. Nobody."

Another time was a guy I knew from home named Shorty. He drove up one Sunday and I intercepted him as soon as he walked through the caddy pen door. "Shorty, you need to turn around and go on home because you're drunk."

He yelled, "I'm tired of you! All the other caddies are scared of you. I ain't scared of your black ass."

The whiskey made him feel brave or stupid. Haven't figured that out yet. I fired him on the spot. Two days later he sent his wife to the course begging for me to give him back his job. A day later he died. He's in that big golf course in the sky.

The Seminole

DADDY TOOK MY HAND and we walked into the backyard to hit balls. At ten years old, he put a six iron in my hand, and I learned the basics of golf. My ability to understand fundamentals came as natural to me as breathing. His instruction paved the way for me to train hundreds of individuals in the sport.

"Danny, the object of the game," he said, "is to get your ball from the tee to the hole in as few shots as possible."

He pointed to a large tree, swollen fruit drooping low, broad leathery leaves bouncing against the breeze. "The hole is the physical circle where the flag resides; it's also the entire area from tee to green." Like the dark expanse of the universe I stared into each night, here too my dreams soared. I felt as alive with a club in my hand as I had while holding a bat.

Driving and chipping and putting balls into the woods became a daily habit. When time to retrieve the balls, I'd hit the bushes with the club to scare away the critters. Always remember, a rat and a snake will retreat long before you reach them if you make loud enough a racket. The same goes for people. If you can't beat them, scare them off with a lot of noise.

Daddy and I began to bond in ways we hadn't yet experienced. I might have stayed in the yard perfecting my stroke all day if I didn't have other obligations. Raking leaves and hauling scrap helped me save pocket change to get those things worth having that Daddy spoke about. We were required to give Mama our earnings no matter the amount. She or Daddy then gave us an age-based allowance.

My pennies added up slow to none. I was ready to dress up like Daddy and my brothers. The hand-me-downs, three-deep and worn. Frustrated I asked, "Mama, how long do I have to wear everybody's old clothes?"

"Danny, you're doing well." Mama pulled me aside as if she were about to tell me a guarded secret. "From now on," she said supportively, "keep two thirds of your money and buy your own clothes."

Caddying was my entry into the world of oxfords and argyles, tailored slacks, and colorful cashmere pull-overs. At twelve, I bought what I wanted. JC Harris, a tailor shop on old Clematis, had fancy shirts and sweaters. I paid ten dollars for a shirt in 1950. That's why I mowed and raked lawns, gutted fish, and caddied.

Daddy was a sharp dresser. He emulated the wealthy men on the course dressed in clothes that made them look rich and important. That appealed to me. My goal in school was to be best dressed and best athlete. I was always the best dresser. As a senior my clothes were tailored. I had two suits: a church suit and a funeral suit.

We carried bags based on how Daddy taught us how to gear up. Hold it here, hold your hand there. We knew to display conduct becoming a gentleman. I was a Tasmanian devil on the course, but I complied on the course, if only long enough to earn a generous tip.

Wise to the ways of the world, Daddy reminded us daily that a job well done brings a sense of personal satisfaction and a feeling of accomplishment no man can take from you. He told us never to lower our head before anyone, to always look a person in the eye. From him I learned what the measure of a man was; to you I share those lessons:

1. Be impeccable with your word. If you say you're going to do something, do it.

2. Stand up for your frailties as boldly as you stand up for your strengths. If I can't do something, I don't do it. Each person on a team has his or her position to play.

3. When your manhood is challenged, you must hold your ground. Stand firm in your beliefs and defend yourself.

4. If you're wrong, admit it. No one is right all the time.

5. Don't be wishy-washy. I am the same yesterday, today, and tomorrow.

6. To thine own self be true. Love who stares back at you in the mirror.

Daddy expected us to pull our weight from an early age. Honeyman and Gene picked tomatoes in summer's blistering heat. In fact, growing up we knew it was either caddy at the Winter Club or catch the bus to Belle Glade and work in the bean or sugar cane fields. For me, that wasn't going to happen.

At ten I was lean and strong, however, Mama objected of me carrying heavy golf bags around all day. I had fallen arches that required special shoes and she thought lugging bags around might make matters worse.

One Saturday early in the season, while Daddy, Mama, and Faye went to Leesburg to bury Granddad, I went to the North Palm Beach Winter Club with my brothers. Wealthy Palm Beach residents came out in droves. Busloads of guests from the Mayflower Hotel descended on area courses like ants on breadcrumbs. Players either dragged a pull cart, carried their own bag, or hired a caddy. There was plenty money to be had for a striving young person willing to work.

This day, the course was in dire need of workers, so the caddy master put me on a bag. I earned my first three dollars as a caddy on a beautiful fall day in 1948. Impressed that a ten-year-old boy knew where to stand, the difference between clubs, could keep up and keep quiet, the guest asked me to return the next day.

It was expected for Daddy and the boys to gather around the table and empty their pockets at the end of a round. Mama counted the money and gave each a share of their earnings. The remainder went to the house. I hadn't contributed up to that point, so I was thrilled to hand Mama my three dollars. Well she liked to have a conniption. "What are you doing letting my little boy go on that course when the bag is bigger than him?" She laid into Gene and Honeyman.

They said, "But Mama, he can do it. They even want him to come back."

I said, "Mama, if Buck can do it, so can I." Even though Buck was two and half years older than me, I thought I could do everything he did and better.

Daddy and my brothers pleaded, and she finally came agreed to let me go out on the weekends and days off from school. I caddied for some of the biggest names in golf from that day on.

I caddied at the Winter Club for most of the 1948-1949 season then I began working at the Seminole with Daddy. When they found out Robert Calloway's son was with him, they gave me a lot of work. I got paid to shag balls, wash clubs, and tidy up the pen. I did this for two years until I began regularly carrying bags.

As I matured, I was put on bags with the bigger personalities. I caddied for more entertainers, business tycoons, and public figures than any other caddy.

The winter of 1961, President Kennedy played the Seminole. The secret service asked the caddy master, Alvin Shellman, to send four of his best caddies. He submitted my name and others for security clearance.

The foursome was the President, television personality Ed Sullivan, Senator George Smathers, and David Reynolds, of Reynolds aluminum foil fame and the member responsible for paying each caddy. I was Reynold's caddy and supported him with authoritative knowledge of the game. We made ten dollars per bag even though five was obligatory.

President Kennedy's detail went far ahead on each hole to survey the area. JFK was not the best golfer. One thing is for sure. I don't care who you are or how much you spend on your clubs, if you don't invest in lessons or practice, you'll remain average. You can't just walk on a golf course and expect to be good.

Before the round, Mr. Sullivan came into the caddy pen making small talk motioning with a swing. "How you boys doing today. I'm Ed Sullivan."

I'll never forget one of the caddies said, "And I'm Harold McIlveen." He was not afraid nor impressed. Mr. Sullivan was a good sport though.

Another time Billy Graham came into the pen. He was in the area conducting a revival and had rare downtime. I admired him because of his revivals and world crusades so I went over to shake his hand and greet him. Tall and gangly, he was just as personable and holy ghost filled as he came across on television. He stood on a grassy knoll overlooking the ocean and said, "I have never played such a beautiful course." He wasn't a skillful player. It was obvious he didn't get out much. He confirmed my observation during a later conversation. I couldn't wait to tell Mama who I had met. She liked Billy Graham too. Meeting him was one of many highlights of my years at the Seminole.

Not every encounter is pleasant. I had a reputation for not taking trash from the caddies nor the members. I was fired for an altercation with a player and was rehired when the boss found out. A member and I were heading to the eighth hole. The rule then was you could leave the flag in the hole or take it out. It was optional. Nowadays the rule is when you reach the green you must take the pin out the hole.

The player will tell you to either tend the pin or leave it in. The man for whom I was caddying didn't tell me one way or the other, so I left the flag in, standing alongside. He putted, the ball hit the pin and rolled past the hole. Had the flag been out he would have holed it and scored a birdie. He said, "You dummy! You didn't see the ball going in?"

I didn't say anything, but I was hot as hades. He called me a dummy, but I know he wanted to call me something else.

He said, "I ought to break your leg for not pulling that pin."

I dropped that pin and stepped toward him. If he had drawn the club back, I'd be in his hip pocket, that's how close I was to him. Sensing a turn of unfortunate events was about to happen, the other members of his foursome rushed over. They said, "Leave that caddy alone; you're wrong." I quit on his bag, walked off the ninth hole, and told Alvin Shellman, the caddy master.

"Mr. Alvin, the man cursed at me and drew his club back," I said. "He got away with it this time. Put someone in my place to finish." This incident occurred before I signed with the Pirates, so I was no more than seventeen, eighteen years old. "If he says something to me again, I will bust his brains out."

I would never let a job dictate my personality or character. These hands could do whatever I tell them to do. I was gonna always have a job. And you don't have to respect me. But what you won't do is mistreat me. Besides, I was on my way to the big league; I didn't need this aggravation. I said my peace and drove home.

Another time, the big cheese of the course, Chris Dunphy, requested me to caddy for him. We got on the eleventh hole, and he asked me, "Dan, what club is this?"

I knew it called for a four wood. I said, "It's a lot of wind up there, let's get the four."

"No, give me my five." He was insistent and did not back down. A good caddy never argues with the player.

In any event, he hit that ball and the wind knocked it down into the lip of the trap. "How'd you let me hit this ball. You knew it was the wrong club. Get off this golf course!"

I didn't mumble a word. I went and told Alvin. I said, "Get my money for ten holes. I'm leaving."

When Mr. Dunphy got off the golf course, he asked, "Where's Danny?"

"He's gone. I'll take his money."

"You have him on my bag tomorrow."

"Didn't you fire him off your bag?"

"Yeah, I told him to get off the golf course, but I won't fire him. I can't play without Danny."

He begged Alvin to find me and put me back on his bag. I went back on it. Mr. Dunphy was a great man to the caddies. He might fuss with us, but he wasn't going to let anyone else do so. We called him Daddy Dunphy. We had to go through him to get anything, but he was great to the guys. He found out I don't hold a grudge, but I won't take any mess either.

One of my least favorite persons was the Duke of Windsor, the king who abdicated his throne so he could marry his lover, Wallis Simpson. No one wanted his bag because he was cheap and didn't tip well.

A good caddy master is lord over his caddies. From dawn to dusk he makes sure the members are well-represented on the course. Raise the flag in the morning, lower it in the evening and in the rain. He earns his keep by being strategic about how he places a particular caddy with a specific member. A member might also come up to the caddy master and ask, "Can I have Calloway today? I've heard how good he is." Alvin might say, "Hmm, it's not his time to go but I'll send him with you." He's sending a message to the member to give me a good tip. The caddies make the caddy master money.

People leave imprints on your mind, good and bad. Members who tip well leave a pleasant impression and you remember who they are, what their preferences are, how high or low their handicap. It is my responsibility to match the perfect caddy to that person. That's where my retention skills come into play. If I know a player has a low handicap, he needs somebody who call the club and greens well. If a man has a bad handicap, I must send a good caddy who can help his game. At the end of a round I ask the player how the caddy performed, and I file it my memory bank.

Benno C. Schmidt Sr., an imposing venture capitalist, might have given the impression he was mean if it weren't for his thoughtful smile. His bushy white eyebrows danced when he spoke of his son, the 20th president of Yale University. Kind to caddies, he always gave them one hundred dollars for his bag and one hundred for his wife's. Then he would give me fifty dollars. Whenever he played, I knew I was getting fifty dollars. And I knew to give him the best caddy.

One of the few women I had the pleasure of meeting was Dinah Shore, singer and show host from the 40s through 70s. She was organizing a big tournament in California and wanted me to go out west and help her with the Dinah Shore Open at Pebble Beach. I told her I couldn't help with the tournament, but I'd be glad to play in it.

I had great relationships with my players. I knew all the terminology and what clubs to use in various conditions. I talked enough but not too much. Members didn't know that was why I excelled as a caddy and I wasn't disclosing it. You had to be careful what you shared with members and guests.

Best of all, I got to walk one of the most beautiful courses in the country that consistently ranked in the top ten. The Seminole was designed in the 1920 as one of the first elite clubs in the lower southern state. Undulating greens, sand dune ridges, and palm tree-lined fairways lay beside the rolling waves of the Atlantic splashing against the sea wall. The Spanish-style clubhouse with its terra cotta roof tiles greets you as you come down the drive. In the locker room gold lettered plaques adorn knotty pine walls, cantilevered wood ceilings vault above mounted moose and deer head.

I caddied for a big lawyer named Paul Otis Sommers. His wife was a descendant of the Hatfield's, the wealthy side of the feud claim to fame. He offered to put me through qualifying school, then I was drafted. When we got away from the clubhouse, he would ask me to play his ball to the hole. His wife said, "Otis, if you just could hit it like that, you'd be all right."

Remember, the courses were segregated. We could caddy but we couldn't play. But that was the type of relationship I had with Mr. Sommers. He was always good to me. When I was a caddy, I should not have played with any member. As caddy master, I could go out for nine holes when there was no work. We stayed in touch over the years. For years, whenever he returned, I was his personal caddy.

When the season slowed, we'd sit on crates outside the pen and wait for assignments. Without fail, one of the regulars, a big steel magnate known for his philanthropy, threw a thousand dollars on the grass and told us to split it among ourselves.

Up until now, my relationship with Whites was spotty at best. Senator Lewis had been the only White adult with whom I had interacted that seemed genuine in his concern for us. But while working at the Seminole my perspective began to change. For sure I met men who couldn't be bothered with us. But we were treated fairly, and most of the members were generous and kind to their caddies.

I've been asked what it was like to caddy for one of the greatest golfers ever to walk tee to green: Ben Hogan. Every year he came down for about month readying for the Masters. When Mr. Sommers wasn't playing, I caddied for Ben.

Initially, I shagged for him. Years ago, there were no driving ranges. When members or their guests practiced, they hit balls into the field, the caddy recovered the balls, and brought them back to the member. We'd do that until they were ready to head to the first tee. Everyone knew I caddied for Mr. Sommers, but Ben would ask the caddy master, "Are you getting Danny out here for me?" I was available for him the better part of the month he was there.

Ben didn't want to be near the clubhouse around the members wives and guests looking for autographs or small talk. We went out on the fourteenth hole or down between the first and ninth tee so we could avoid everyone.

On the course he was all business, cigarette hanging from his mouth, trademark white hat on his head. Ten years and he didn't speak more than a thousand words to me. On my hand-me-down school baseball jacket was the name "Chuck," so he assumed that was my name. He never asked my name but called me Chuck for the entire time I caddied for him.

Precise, he could hit the ball straight down the middle of the fairway every time. As an athlete who marvels at the greats in every sport—Michael Jordan, Willie Mays, Joe Louis—he's on my Rushmore. You can't talk about Arnold Palmer, Jack Nicklaus, Tiger Woods, without mentioning Ben Hogan.

He was an outstanding golfer who knew what he needed to do to win. His concentration was unbelievable. He preferred to walk so he could think about his next shot. That's how mentally prepared he was. When we got to the ball, he'd ask me," What is it, a five or a six?" He knows it's one of the two but looked for me to validate. "Get the five, its wind up there," I'd say. He needed my opinion to validate his decision.

Hogan's ball dropped on the grass like a butterfly with soft feet. His steely blue-green eyes watched the ball land exactly where he meant for it to sit. If he were a better putter, he might have had more victories than Sam Sneed, Tiger, and Nicklaus. He paid ten dollars per bag when everyone else was paying five. The more I learned about the game, the more I appreciated how good he really was.

On the other hand, Arnold Palmer didn't talk to me much. I will never know if it was because I was Black, or if he was just a snooty player. Nonetheless, he was never friendly with me. Most player-caddy relationships perform like team play; it's you and him against the field. I didn't drink or smoke. I studied every green. I knew everything the player and caddy should do.

I had the privilege of carrying bags for many of the great golfers of my time. Some were stiff-necked; others thought I was the best thing that almost happened. Besides, I was a student of human nature. I knew when someone didn't like me, and they knew when I didn't like them, which was rare. Like I said, I'm an open book. I wear my heart on my sleeve. Arnold and I simply didn't mesh. I didn't caddy for him too often.

The Golden Bear, Jack Nicklaus, invited me up Sunday afternoon at Benjamin Gym where a bunch of white athletes played basketball. They played rough because they were slow. They could shoot but it wasn't for me. I only caddied for Jack on a practice round, but he taught me something I never forgot.

We were on a par five. His second shot was a tight lie, but he wanted to knock it on in three and put for eagle.

"Danny, what do think it is?"

"You gonna need three wood to get there but I think it's best for you to hit the four wood because your ball is on a tight lie."

"Danny don't ever tell a professional golfer why he should use a certain club. Just tell him what club you think is the right club and nothing more."

He was right. A professional can hit a ball off any lie. I didn't need to tell him why. But then again, I was talking to him like I was caddying for a member or his guest. They expected me to tell them what and why. I would never let a member play badly if I could help it. I was like their coach. That's why I liked the position so much. It was a teacher student relationship. If I said, "no, don't hit that," they wouldn't hit that. "To get it there, hit this, you'll have a margin of error." And they'd hit this to get it there. Members requested me because I understood and had a deep respect for the game.

I loved instructing. It came as natural to me as breathing and eating. Remember, I was the first Black certified instructor at Montauk Downs. I took immense pride in learning everything I could from club pros. I passed on what I learned to the members. That was why I gravitated toward Charlie Sifford. First, he was willing to share with me what he knew. Second, I held my own against him.

I visited Doc's ex-wife in Texas during a time when she and her team planned for the annual Prairie View Alumni Golf Tournament in Houston. Susan, an executive at the bank, was chair of the tournament that year. The group she worked with on the planning committee suggested Charlie Sifford be the Grand Marshall. They racked their brains over who to place in his foursome. You don't normally put players in a foursome who can beat the star in the group. You always want the big man to win. Susan suggested me; Charlie agreed.

"You sure you want him in your foursome?" a member asked him. "I know you can beat him, but we don't want him to hold up play either."

"Hold on now," Charlie said. "I've played Dan many times and he's matched me stroke for stroke."

"You mean to tell me he's that good?"

"That's what I mean to tell you; he's that good."

I planned my trip to support the alumni event in Houston. Eight days before the event I was told that Susan and her partner were involved in a bad accident. Her car went over a viaduct and killed her instantly. I didn't play in the tournament.

I first met Charlie Sifford when he and his wife Rose wintered in Florida. He spent two or three months thawing out from the frigid, Cleveland winters in the tepid winds of West Palm Beach. Charlie was the first Black to ever win a tournament, first Black to win the Masters, and the first Black pro given a golf course in Cleveland, Ohio.

Every Friday he stopped by our house for a hot fish dinner. He didn't care to talk all night to Daddy about golf, and I was tasked with keeping the conversation from veering too far left. Cigar in mouth we'd talk about life and the pursuit of happiness. To be honest, he didn't even want to talk about that. All Charlie wanted was a hot, crispy red snapper fried on the bone.

When he became club pro, I often stayed with him and Rose in Cleveland between trips from New York and Detroit and he and I played many rounds. Good golfers want to play against other good golfers. That's the beauty of competition no matter the sport. When I played high school ball, I always wanted to play the teams that forced me to be a better player. When you play inferior athletes, which sometimes you do, you don't have to push yourself past a certain level. You don't have to stretch. But when I played Charlie at his course, Shaky Heights, it was always a competitive match.

When I was chosen to caddy in the 1972 PGA Championship in Palm Beach Gardens, the same dynamic was at play. In those days you couldn't bring your own caddy. You had to use someone local. Each golf course selected the best caddies to attend. I graded better than anyone in Palm Beach County. Then, I was placed with a pro out of Birmingham, Michigan. He was a terrible golfer making awful shots. I was upset he wasn't doing better. The last day I said, "You should be carrying the bag for me and I should be playing. I could have done better than you."

He knew he had played a disaster of a round. "Dan," he said. "You probably would have done better."

I couldn't wait for the round to end. I took off four days from the Sherriff's office for this mess.

That reminded me of the times Daddy carried the bag for Gracie Emery, one of the top amateurs in the country. She was an outstanding golfer who loved to bet on her rounds against some of the top names in golf if they gave her enough strokes. She waited to see who performed the worse and then she'd try to get them to spot her strokes. That was her strategy and it worked. She beat them often and pocketed a lot of money too.

I liked Gracie. She was crazy about Robert Calloway Sr., regularly giving us money to slip to Daddy when he refused to accept it from her directly. When Daddy was laid off, she bought us clothes and food. It was people like Gracie that got me to change my perspective on communities outside my own. Not because of what she had done for us, but because I knew she was sincere. Likened to a good caddie, you can tell if one is serious by the way she carries the bag.

Gracie's husband and club president, Mr. Ryan sent for me when the caddies got out of control and no longer up to form. In 1979 I had been three years in law enforcement when Mr. Ryan called for me to become caddy master. Frankly, outside of professional baseball, that would have been my dream job. But because the Sheriff's Department had already invested a lot of money in my training and education, I couldn't just quit. Besides, the Seminole was only six months out the year and, at the time, provided no paid time off, insurance, or a pension.

I had to decide: refuse my dream job at the Seminole, or stay in Riviera with my two sons, be a part of their lives, keep up with them in school, guarantee myself insurance and a pension for life. If I took the caddy master job it meant six months in

Florida and six months in New York. I'd have two households and more expenses. But it also meant I would make four, five times what I earned in the Sheriff's Office. I couldn't do it to my boys. At the time they were still in school and needed a father figure to guide and love them.

It was a tough decision, but I stayed with the Sheriffs Office. I also became a caddy master two years after I graduated from the Police academy. The Seminole never had an assistant caddy master, so I hired my friend, Ernest Johnson, to run the pen five days and I'd come up on the weekends. It was a full-time job, but I didn't leave the department. I wanted the pension. Some days I showed up to the course in a three-piece suit and holster. My sons, Darryl and Ray came with me sometimes and I'd let them work. They earned a lot of money and got the caddying bug.

I carried bags for forty-eight years, eleven of which I served as Caddy Master. Those two positions were the most rewarding jobs I've ever had. At least forty caddies worked under me every day. It was I who determined whether they went on the course or not. If they slept in dirty clothes, smelled like liquor, or didn't control their mouth, they didn't go out.

I won't have a player telling me one of my guys is not doing his job. Some of the best deals in the world are made on the golf course. One of my caddies will not get in the way of a successful business transaction. If a player says something to you, be ready to answer. But don't run your mouth so much so that the player can't hear himself think.

I earned a master's degree on the golf course and learned aspects of stroke play that transcend the sport. Golf is a silent game, played between the ears, and on constant replay. It's a mental game that can get away from you before you realize what happened. A caddie must know when to calm his or her player down. Never tell a player or his guest, "That's a bad shot." You must always be positive. "The wind got it. You just missed it. You'll get the next one." You always want to be encouraging.

Golf is mental. It can get away from you in no time. You have to know when to walk off and let the player stew a little. The next hole you might want to say something. Make the player feel like he wasn't himself. You never get into an arguing match with your player. If they pick a club that you know is wrong, encourage them by saying, "Stay with it. It's a good one."

I expected my caddies to have the utmost professionalism at all times. This was not a democracy. I ran a dictatorship and if they had a problem with that they could leave. They worked at the whims of Dan Calloway.

I could tell if a new caddy would perform his job well by the way he picked up the bag as well as how he placed it down. The bag is supposed to swing on your shoulder and tilt across your back over your lower hip. That's one bag. If you're carrying two bags, one bag is on each shoulder you're your right hand over the heads of the bag with the bags parallel to the ground. There are tell-tell mannerisms one displays when he swings the bag over his shoulder.

I started a Junior Caddy program at every Golf club for which I work to provide honest labor for adolescents while they learn the fundamentals of golf and the life skills associated with such an exciting game. Darryl and Ray and six other children participated in the program.

Most jobs I had the latitude to do what I wanted within the parameters of the job for which I was hired. But you have got to trust me. You must have faith in your decision to hire me because if you have a problem with anything I do, expect me to stand my ground. I will never wimp out or back down.

When hired, I let everybody know if there arose a problem with any of my caddies or invited guests, please allow me to take care of it. I told them from the beginning that I was one Black man they weren't accustomed to, that they couldn't handle me any old way. I came as a man and I will leave as one.

Clark crabbed in the lake when the greenskeeper harassed him for being there. I said, "Look Bill, I asked you to come to me if you had a problem with anyone who comes on the course."

Still with the Sherriff's office, I had the authority to diffuse any conflict that I considered explosive. Also, I was still the caddie master; bring it to my attention. I got mad. I felt he disrespected me. "I tell you what," I said to Bill. "You ought to be glad I don't take a two wood and bust you over the head." He reported me to the Club President.

At the end of the year, I received a letter firing me. "You've been a magnificent employee, but we have to part ways since you can't work with others and are too confrontational." Alan Rhine hired me. George Coleman's godson fired me.

Ten years as caddie master on those hallowed grounds, I earned my spurs; but my greatest moment was when one of the wealthiest members of the club invited me to play. I was the first Black man to play as a guest at the Seminole. The caddies came out the pen cheering and clapping.

I retired from the Sherriff's Office in 1997. I continued to caddy for some of my regular clients, many of whom became good friends over the years.

HITS AND MISSES

The Little Leagues

JOE LOUIS DEFENDED HIS heavyweight title against Billy Conn at Yankee Stadium in 1946, and I was glued to the radio, clinging to the broadcaster's every word. The highly prized match was the first televised World Heavyweight Championship bout ever. At eight, I realized the brevity of the moment.

From my living room floor, ear pressed against the speaker, it felt as if I were sitting ringside. When Louis was interviewed, he said, "He can run, but he can't hide." His words stoked a fire in me that burns to this day. I jumped for joy when the Brown Bomber retained his crown with a knockout in the eighth round.

Every Saturday night, the family gathered around the radio to listen to "The Hit Parade," sponsored by Phillip Morris. The boy, in an accentuated drawl announced, "Call Phillip Morris." I thought it was the funniest thing ever.

Hopalong Cassidy and Popeye the Sailor Man became childhood idols to many boys. Listening to the radio inspired us to dream about being heroes who saved the day. It encouraged us to believe in what was possible. For most children, the radio was our church.

A lot of my friends wanted to be cowboys like the Lone Ranger and Gene Autry. They dreamt about things heard over

141

the radio and read in books. Because so many children emulated Autry, he created the Cowboy Commandments:

1. The Cowboy must never shoot first, hit a smaller man, or take unfair advantage.
2. He must never go back on his word, or a trust confided in him.
3. He must always tell the truth.
4. He must be gentle with children, the elderly, and animals.
5. He must not advocate or possess racially or religiously intolerant ideas.
6. He must help people in distress.
7. He must be a good worker.
8. He must keep himself clean in thought, speech, action, and personal habits.
9. He must respect women, parents, and his nation's laws.
10. The Cowboy is a patriot.

Of course, one can't be certain if these rules were for children like me. In any event, when systems are put in place to promote moral conduct and values and they produce good for all when followed, they are important to have. Codes of conduct are important for keeping order and law. However, not all rules and laws are fair.

Jim Crow laws, under Florida state constitution, mandated legal segregation in public facilities and spaces. That included schools, hospitals, movies, restaurants, bathrooms. The rules of law upheld under the United States Supreme Court's doctrine of "separate but equal," served to conquer an unconquerable people.

At one time, Black men made up to a quarter of the population of cowboys. They faced the same discrimination in towns they rode through like Black men in the south and were barred from public spaces, hotels, and restaurants.

Bill Pickett was the best-known Black cowboy and rodeo performer in the early twentieth century. He had the unique skill of grabbing cattle by the horns and wrestling them to the ground which spearheaded the technique of "bulldogging."

Most of the kids I played beside wanted to be either a cowboy or heavy weight champ. I loved boxing, but my favorite pastime was listening to the game of the week. I wanted to win the pennant.

We played stick ball two blocks from the house in an open dirt field; no gloves, no shirts, no shoes. The McGaney-owned property bordered woods and a two-bedroom house with overgrown lawn. Neighborhood kids gathered on the lot eager to show their skills. Captains tossed a coin and picked their teammates. Anxious kids shuffled the dust waiting to be chosen. We used rocks or shirts for bases. Sometimes we drew a circle in the dirt. Whatever the case, it was the best training ground I could have ever had.

At eleven I played league ball. In 1950 David Fields, Riviera Beach's first Black police officer, went to the Kiwanians and got us blue and gold uniform tops. We still played barefoot wearing dungarees but at least we looked like a team.

He told us, "Boys, you are now the Riviera Eagles and we're going to compete in an eight-team league in West Palm Beach."

This was the first time a team out of the woods ever competed in league play. Up to that point it was sandlot ball. We didn't have a real baseball field in Riviera until Mr. Lewis bought land, cleaned it up, and put a fence around.

We played our first League game on that field against Walter Walker, a pitcher known for his fast, powerful straight balls which struck out most kids. He was so muscular and strong we called him Samson. His teammate Richard Mitchell told him to not go easy on me, assuring him I was good. "That boy can hit."

First up to bat, Walter fueled the ball toward me with gale force. I ripped it past his ears far into center field and ran the bases to third. Richard yelled, "I told you not to take it easy on him!"

"I didn't take it easy…he just hit the darn ball!"

I jumped up and down taunting him to high heaven. "Don't throw mess like that to me," I said, daring him to come for me. I had to establish myself as either an unflappable, fearless opponent or a pompous fool. Sometimes you have to prove yourself to keep from getting pushed around. Other times you must prove only to yourself that you have what it takes to win.

It would have been a perfect game but Frank Garvin, a left-hand batter bunted the ball in front of the plate. I ran for it but Cuda Joe grabbed the ball and threw it high and wide. We didn't play six innings, we played nine.

Palm Beach Times had a write-up in the sports page when I struck out twenty-seven batters. I was playing for the West Palm Beach Little League. Charlie Smith put me out my position because he said I was too good. He thought it unfair to the other players to never have the chance to hit a ball.

Growing up, I mimicked centerfield players like Hank Aaron and Joe DiMaggio, and studied their every move. Whether I pitched or played centerfield, I anticipated whether the ball was going to my right or left. Good judgment in sports is necessary. Daddy once told me, "don't show your hand," and I haven't ever since.

Our toughest match loomed on the horizon. We had won seven games and were headed for the eighth. The championship match, held at Lincoln Park in West Palm Beach, looked like ours for the taking. Before we got up to bat, the organizer disqualified us for being out of uniform. We cried for some time to come.

Our manager asked," Why are you disqualifying us?"

"Your players don't have on shoes."

"But you let us play the other games. We have never worn shoes and we've won seven games."

He walked away with no further explanation, heartlessly robbing us of our chance to prove ourselves league champion. He judged us because we were shoeless, woodland players from Riviera. Bad enough we had to fight whites on the other side of the tracks for looking different. But we had to fight our own for living in the woods.

Turns out the referee's friend had brought a team up from Ft. Lauderdale. We had the winningest record and the best players, but the ref wanted his friend's team to win. That taught me two things:

1. There are those willing to win at any cost and will
2. People cheat

That disqualification fueled a fire under me to outplay, outsmart and be better than anyone, showing that even wood boys were good enough to win under any circumstance. People put us down for coming from where we came from. I had a chip on my shoulder, even though Mama and Daddy told us to hold up our heads and be proud of who we were and what we had.

Our manager couldn't spell baseball let alone put together a team strategy or keep us from being disqualified. We never had an adult to teach us fundamentals. Evidenced by my school team play, I was appointed coach, even though younger than half the team. I trained my inexperienced teammates using what I had learned from books and playing daylong with older boys. I coached league teams every summer throughout high school until I signed with the Pirates which helped pave the way to my future as a coach.

Jackie Robinson All-Stars

WHEN JACKIE ROBINSON BROKE the baseball color line on April 15, 1947 to become the first Black man to play Major League Baseball, I knew instantly I would be a professional ball player. Everything Jackie Robinson did, I did. I read about him in books and magazines, I discussed his stats with my friends. I rushed home from school to listen to the game of the week on the radio. It didn't matter what else was going on in the world, my ear was pinned to the radio. Except on Sundays.

During baseball season, after church the whole town came out in the heat of the afternoon to watch the Riviera Tigers play. Adults cooked fish and chicken in boil pots, roasted peanuts in tins, and sold big bottles of RC cola. Today it's called tailgating; then it was called community.

In 1948 the team asked me to be bat boy. I was ten years old and jumped at the chance to learn from veteran players. Mama told them, "Just give him a ball and he'll be happy."

Was I too naïve to believe that this wide-eyed boy who played stick ball on unpaved country roads could be what he wanted to be? I practiced being the best from the best because I wanted to do what they did, but better.

Mama kept every book and magazine at my disposal. Bob Feller's book taught me all about pitching. I had to know how

147

he became a Hall of Famer. Batting techniques I learned by mimicking Ted Williams, one of the greatest hitters who ever lived. I devoured books. Daddy and I went down to the field to watch the professional baseball teams during spring training.

I saw my future clear as you see this page. There was nothing that could cause me to deviate from the vision I held of myself. See, it's one thing to say you want to do this or that. But it's an entirely different thing to say, "I did that." When I make up my mind to do something, I plan the work then work the plan. I cross every T and dot every I. Even when faced with obstacles, if you stay determined, mountains move. I stayed true to my vision of playing pro ball and, at fourteen years of age, played against two of the biggest names in baseball.

In 1952 I was lead-off hitter for the Riviera Tigers when Jackie Robinson's Allstars barnstormed in West Palm Beach. My family and what seemed half the town came out to see if I, a wood boy from Riviera, could withstand the pressure and stand tall before giants of the game.

It was oppressively humid; my hands, clammy and tight. I looked the pitcher up and down and studied his hands for signs. A good hitter knows what's coming; it's all in the fingers. Since I was the greatest pitcher to hit Palm Beach County, I knew exactly what to look for: fingers straight over top, fastball. Ball wedged between forefinger and thumb: curve. I spit beside the plate, choked up on the bat, and waited to make history.

On the mound was the great Satchel Paige, an aging Hall of Famer still proving his mettle. The tall, lanky right hander struck me out with a fastball first time up to bat. Cool Papa Bell once said, "Satchel could throw the ball by your knees all day," and that's exactly what he did as he struck me out the second time. The third time I got up to bat I said, "This old man ain't striking me out three times." Well, Satchel blew it by me. I walked off the field so dejected I could have cried.

Humiliated, yes. And yet, it was the best thing ever to happen to me. Nothing compared to this fourteen-year-old playing with some of the greats of the game. Satchel walked up to me and shook my hand. He didn't know how young I was. How could he? I was playing with grown men. Jackie Robinson walked over to me, put his hand on my shoulder and said, "Little man. You did well. You're going to be all right."

Five-time Hall of Fame inductee, multimillion-dollar complex bearing my name, travelled internationally, sat with Presidents, but Jackie Robinson's words meant more than a lot. To this day I refer to that game as one of the highlights of my life. Turned out to be the best day of my life. But that was the last time I'd ever get outmatched like that.

I went home, trained hard every day, determined to up my game. Losses never came easy for me. I had to win, whether it was playing or coaching. That loss showed me I still had a long way to go. Better still, it taught me I wasn't going to win every game no matter how good I thought I was.

Jackie Robinson was invited to Roosevelt High school as guest speaker at an assembly. The school piled into the auditorium to hear what this soft-spoken hero had to say. I hung on to his every word, but two things resonated most.

First, he said, "I'm not concerned with your liking or disliking me...all I ask is that you respect me as a human being." Then, he said, "A life is not important except in the impact it has on other lives." The room quieted. No one wanted him to leave. As he moved from the lectern, a rumble of applause filled the room.

His words felt familiar, almost stolen. I never cared whether someone liked me or not. If you don't like me, that's your problem. I like myself. Those of us who work to make a difference in the lives of the least, the fruit they bear will be proof as to whether we've left a lasting impact.

I didn't get to meet him after the talk, but I already had the pleasure of meeting him on one of the worse and best days of my life.

The Negro League

I PITCHED FOR THE Riviera Tigers and played centerfield for the Kansas City Monarchs. My high school coach didn't want me to pitch with them for fear I'd hurt my arm before I signed with the league. Everyone knew I was headed to the majors.

Bob Mitchell, another Roosevelt High graduate who pitched with the Monarch's from 1954-1957 told me these words, "Don't get yourself hooked up with the Negro League; you gonna make 'the show.'" In other words, he, like my high school coach and half the town, knew I was headed for the Majors.

Most of the big names like Willie Mayes, Hank Aaron, Jackie Robinson, all played "black baseball" before they signed with a major league team. But hundreds more never made it into organized ball or "the big league." The riotous decade following Robinson breaking the color line, most MLB teams signed only one or two Black players at a time. To be frank, many of the truly phenomenal players were old before they were ever allowed to play in the major leagues; they were in the sunset of their lives.

What most people don't realize is that long before the charter of the Negro American League in 1937, Blacks and Whites played on the same teams. The teams weren't segregated until the start of the twentieth century. When Jackie Robinson broke the color line, he actually re-integrated the leagues.

At its height, the Negro Leagues crowded families into stadiums across the country, including Palm Beach County, provided Blacks with their own American pastime.

The Tigers played all over Florida. Because I had no contract or agent, I could play with any team that called, sometimes on the road for weeks at a time. We travelled by bus from one city to the next, bathing in the bus station, walking through back doors of restaurants that served us. Most of the men told me I could do better.

At fourteen, I played on the Recreation Department's Junior league. The Colt League ranged in age from nineteen to twenty-two. The league's leftfielder got hurt and the manager allowed me to come up from the Junior team. The kids on the team were four and five years older than me.

I played centerfield on the West Palm Beach Indians alongside two of my brothers. Buck was a left-handed pitcher who didn't played better in the kitchen than on the field, even though he was the biggest physical. Honeyman was leftfielder. Reverend Jack Rountree played right field. Willie Bow Davis, third most talented on the field, played third. Reverend Jimmie Rountree, the oldest, was at shortstop.

Clifford Monroe was at second. Loyal Daniel Wiley, the best all-around hitter with immense power. The captain/catcher Frank Williams, whose attitude kept everyone in line and in sync, completed the lineup. He was our natural cleanup hitter.

We had a few pinch hitters that came off the bench when needed.

The Pittsburg Pirates

STRAIGHT OUT OF SCHOOL in the summer of 1956 I signed with the Pittsburg Pirates. I had just turned eighteen and was ready for my closeup. I had dreamed of becoming a professional baseball player from the time Jackie Robinson broke the baseball color line.

I got a signing bonus of four thousand dollars which I gave to Mama and Daddy. Even working twelve-hour days, Daddy had yet to make that much in a year. As a rookie who successfully completed camp, I'd earn six to eight thousand a year. That was a lot of money for an eighteen-year-old wood boy in mid-century America, especially when you consider the average family earned just over three thousand dollars annually.

The year I graduated high school it cost fifty cents to see a movie at the Grand. Fifteen cents bought a loaf of bread, thirty cents a gallon of gas. A pair of Converse cost under ten dollars. Life was good.

Three weeks before training camp, I was shooting pool in Baby Mill's poolroom, a smoke-filled, five-tabled dingy hole in the wall. Eighteen years old, five hundred dollars in my pocket, and headed to the show; I was the big man in the room. A pimp named Ham, his stepson LC, a hustler, a drunk, and my friend Clark were shooting high-stakes dice in a corner of the room. I gave Clark my five hundred to put with his two. In less than half an hour he turned our seven hundred dollars into more than three thousand.

"Let's go." We had quadrupled our money and it was time to walk away.

"Naw man, let me throw a few more," Clark insisted, sure he could double what he had already won.

Well, Ham felt cheated and tipped off the police. Ten minutes later four police officers kicked down the door, guns drawn, yelling, "You niggers better not move, or we'll blow your heads off." Guns pointed at us they said, "Put your hands behind your backs."

Thousands of dollars on the floor disappeared. We never saw a penny. They put me, Clark, and LC into the backseat of a cruiser and headed downtown to the county jail. Halfway there, the chief looked in the rearview mirror and asked, "Aren't you Robert Calloway's boy, the one heading to the Majors?"

"Yes sir," I said.

Everyone knew I had signed with the Pirates. My name and picture had been in all the local papers. I was a frequent topic of conversation in every circle: Black, White, rich, poor. I was like a local hero. I should have been more careful, but back then, I thought I was invincible.

"Well boy, your daddy gonna be mighty upset at you."

When we got to the jail, the chief told me to stay in the car while he took Clark and LC inside. Clark had the nerve to suggest, "Tell him I'm your brother so I can go too."

I said, "I'm not gonna tell him that lie. I told you it was time to go. Now, somebody's' got to be punished for the crime."

All the while I was laughing under my breath. It was a joke to me. I wanted to see him sweat. Nevertheless, I had saved ninety-eight dollars which I took out my coat pocket when I got home. I put it with money Clark had, and in the morning took his mother down to the station so she could get all over him. As we bailed Clark out the county jail, I told the chief, "I know you're going to tell my Daddy, but I don't want the people to know I've been arrested for shooting dice."

"Well, we'll try to keep it out the paper," he said.

Next day my name, along with the others, was in the paper. Even though I hadn't been arrested, my name still appeared before the world as a stain on my family's good name. The fact that Mama saw her son's name in the paper for his involvement in a gambling raid hurt like Delta blues.

"Danny, I can't believe you of all people. How could you risk your dream?" Once again, I let Mama down. I could never make it up to her. Mama forgave once more.

I didn't realize it at the time, but I was given a second chance. The police chief didn't arrest me, he took me home to my Daddy. That's why I stand up for people. If you are innocent, I have to stand up for you. But you can be guilty too, and I'll ask for leniency. I'll beg on the mercy of the courts on your behalf. Some people just need a second chance. We all succumb to the temptations of life. No one is perfect.

Fortunately, that bad press didn't affect my contract, and in January 1957 I went to spring training in Jacksonville. For six weeks we'd train with all the big-league teams: Yankees, Cardinals, Red sox, Dodgers. After drills one day, the owners called a meeting with all the Black players, including Roberto Clemente, one of the greatest outfielders of all time.

"We can only carry two colored boys," they said. "Don and Roberto."

I was prepared to play in one of the farm leagues until I got my shot, and I persisted undeterred. Besides, I was training with some of the best players who ever competed and making three hundred dollars a month to boot. What could be better?

As we prepared to play an intersquad game, the manager signaled he needed infielders. Listed on my scouting report was every position but catcher, so they placed me on third. Clemente was in right field, Frank Thomas in left. Dick Groat was shortstop.

A ball was hit to right field. Roberto Clemente strong-armed the ball to third just outside the baseline. I shouldn't have gone for the ball, but I was eager to show off my talents, so I ran to make the tag and Frank hammered into me like a cannon ball. The force bowled me to the ground where I lay momentarily stunned. I was in terrible pain up and down my right side but didn't realize to what extent until I was injured until I stood. I could barely move my arm. My shoulder dislocated. But I continued to play. I didn't tell the manager I was hurt.

My roommate, Don Clendenon, power-hitting first baseball and 1969 World Series MVP, urged me to tell the trainer. I was eighteen years old and had never second-guessed my decisions before. I knew I'd heal. Besides, if I told trainer, they might send me home and I didn't want to disappoint my parents and siblings. I was the first Black in Palm Beach County to sign a professional athletic contract. A newspaper article had called me the next Willie Mays. I carried the hopes of an entire town. Nope; couldn't risk it.

I continued to train and made the injury worse. When the manager found out I was hurt I was put in the Triple A with plans to send me to their farm club in New Orleans. I was denied entrance because it was part of the southern league, which was still segregated. I became expendable. A season ending injury thwarted my dreams. Cut. Disappointed, I hopped aboard the Greyhound and headed home to face the music.

During my senior year of school, I was offered scholarships to colleges of my choice. Everyone wanted me. But I had dreamed of playing professional baseball. I spent sleepless nights gazing through holes in the tar paper from a bed of rags and hope, batting stars into eternity, watching my dreams take flight. When I signed with the Pirates, I could no longer benefit from scholarship money. Broke and injured, college was out.

I had received every award imaginable for my triumphs on the field and court. I had a winning record as a pitcher. Life had thrown me a curve ball. Batter up.

THE BEAT

The Berlin Crisis

PRESIDENT JOHN FITZGERALD KENNEDY conscripted 60,000 men in the 1961 Berlin Crisis which started when the USSR demanded the withdrawal of armed forces from Berlin.

I registered for the draft on Clematis Street in West Palm Beach the year I graduated high school. Six years later, while caddying in New York I received by mail a letter saying Uncle Sam was ready to talk to me. I drove Sellaway's car home and had about two weeks to get myself together before I reported for duty on October 3, 1961.

Two weeks passed and I caught the train to Miami with forty-four scared, excited, and confused young men for a physical and aptitude test. I had so many sports injuries I didn't think I was going to be drafted. I had a pin in my left knee, a previously broken ankle, a bad shoulder, and a gold-capped front tooth. Didn't matter. My aptitude score was higher than everyone in the room. "We'll find a job for you."

We shipped out to Fort Jackson in Columbia, South Carolina where there were so many draftees, they had to open two additional bases. I was shipped to Fort Chaffee, Arkansas and then to Fort Dix, where we would, after training, fly over the Atlantic to Germany. While in New Jersey, they recommended

I go to Officer Candidate School because I scored high on the aptitude test.

"Yeah I'll go." I was excited at the prospect of not having to slog through the mud and snow for drills. "Sounds good."

"Okay, sign here and we'll get you started."

Unaware I'd have to sign up for an additional year to take advantage of officer training, my balloon deflated. I had turned twenty-four the August prior to my draft. That meant I was at least five or six years older than a lot of the boys leaving for the war. That might have worked in my favor, but for me, there remained a huge unknown, so I opted out of officer training.

I disliked basic training. It's a miracle I made it through hell week. Every morning the drill sergeant called roll at formation and the platoon marched out with a traditional call-and-response. I had two left feet; no rhythm. I never got the one, two, three, hut; eyes right, column left, column right, hut, hut of military cadence. The marches were very precise. Remember, I wasn't a dancer; I never learned the boogie woogie. I was an athlete. The only rhythm I had was a pitch and swing, as fluid and graceful as a danseur.

During the tortuous second eight, or advanced training in Paduka, Kentucky, I hated it even more. Drill sergeants continued to holler in face and ear, every move monitored and corrected. I thought Black recruits were singled out because they treated us so badly. Blinded by rage, I couldn't see the sergeants were doing the same thing to others. Everyone took a beating.

I sent letters to my Congressman, the NAACP, and Mama, accusing the corps of racism. I complained to the doctor of old injuries. I was relentless in my appeals. I pitched such a fit they assigned me as a permanent barrack orderly. Every day I stayed in the barracks. I obeyed the law of the land and never broke the rules. I would not allow myself to be dishonorably discharged and bring shame to Mama. I didn't get a response from Washington or the NAACP. Mama reminded me that joy comes in the morning.

Fort Chaffee, Fort Smith Arkansas outside of Eda, Oklahoma: the worst place I've ever been. We had liberty passes to leave the base after four weeks of training so went into town. Businesses wouldn't serve me a glass of water let alone a bottle of coca cola alongside white soldiers just because I was Black. I had been in New York golfing with men of every ilk and yet in uniform I'm ignored and despised. If I couldn't eat, the guys refused to eat. That pleased me.

I took them to a Black-owned spot known for whiting dinners and blues. We walked into mud-splashed floors and flies buzzing around an open garbage can, smelling of spoiled fish. Far worse than the grimiest juke joint in West Palm Beach, I felt so embarrassed. My experience was so bad I didn't leave the base again until they sent me to New Jersey.

It was bitter cold when we arrived at Rhine Main, and quite a shock for a Floridian. Snow melted on the wide walkways. For the past five years I had wintered in Florida on the raised greens of Seminole and summered on the shore in Montauk. This for me was akin to culture shock.

I worked for the General in Special Services, the U.S. military entertainment arm. The War Department created the unit, using specially trained troops to provide recreational and entertainment programs and activities. I was tasked with organizing programs for intramurals, participating in or teaching baseball, football, basketball, and golf. The division was one of the few integrated U.S. Army units during World War II. Everyone thought I was in hog-heaven.

Headquartered in Heidelberg, one of my jobs was to talk to families about the unit's programs, similar to a physical education teacher. I wore civilian clothes, lived on base, ate in the mess hall. But in Special Services I made less per week than I made per day as the caddy master at Montauk. I couldn't wrap my head around that.

Head of the unit, I had a budget, recording and travelling secretary. We caught the train sometimes to neighboring countries that hosted games and events. A lot of the European nations are so small you could visit five countries in one day, similar to the states here.

I had a chance to see sights that I might not have seen if I weren't in the armed services. Kaiserslautern, or K-Town, a US military community twice the population of Riviera Beach, housed Black and White together. It was a beautiful thing to see. The pungency of boiled hops filled the air on the border of France at Zweibrücken.

I went to the Tower of Pisa, a freestanding bell tower in Pisa, Italy. You read about these places in books, but you can't appreciate their grandeur until you see them up close. I

166

ventured off to the French Riviera in the southeast corner of France. Cities along this stretch of the Mediterranean serve as home and playground to the wealthy and boast some of the finest architecture in the world. London had soupy air. That's where I started to drink coffee and Ovaltine because I was always cold. Mr. McDonald was right. There is a big world out here.

Some German towns had as much bigotry as the Jim Crowe states in America. I was in a bar one night with a few friends when two women came over talking and flirting their way to a drink. They had an alluring, yet childish curiosity about them. After an hour, they tittered and asked, "Can we see where your tails were cut off?" If it wasn't so pathetic it would have been funny. In fact, we did laugh; but we didn't show them the scar.

Each base has their own team and the Seventh Army Support Command had some of the worse players ever. I overhauled the team; kept the good ones and recruited fresh blood. We kept our bodies in top form with practice two times per day. Run a few hours after breakfast, shoot around, rest, repeat.

At 6'1" most of the team was tall as me or shorter. We didn't have the height, but we could run and jump. We played a lot of pickup games on the base which provided good practice for the official games. We ended up with an outstanding group of players.

I didn't start out coaching. Sargent Dudley was a lifer and a drinker. He was an older gentleman, but the game had passed him by. I spoke to him about the importance of having a winning team for the morale of the group. He had seen my file and knew I was an all-star player. Fortunately, he knew his contributions had been subpar. As team captain, he gave me the go ahead to coach the team. I became a player/coach.

On paper it looked like Dudley trained the team, but he really sat back and basked in the glory. That was fine by me. I told him to stay drunk and dream of retirement. General Hall learned I coached the teams and appointed me the first Black manager of the baseball team. I let him know if he wanted us to be the best, he had to cut out the jobs. The Air Force teams were as good as they were because they did nothing but practice and train all day. Their job was the position they held on the team. To compete equally, my guys had to do the same.

I had the tenacity and desire to win and I wanted to create a space that allowed men to develop a sense of pride for the unit. My team disciplined themselves, practiced hard, and honed their skills. I competed all my life and I knew what it took to win. Don't get me wrong, there were dynamic players on good teams. A few talented players were drafted into professional leagues. But they didn't have me leading the charge.

Most point guards are coachlike on the floor. They call plays, get instructions from the bench, and pass info to players. Being on the floor as point guard/coach, that means I can yell out the play at the last moment. I don't have to look over to the bench and ask coach what he wants me to run. I'm already on the court. That's where I exceled. I averaged a triple double, again.

Some of my guys could rival the best professionals. Earl Wiley, 6′3″ with thick round glasses was reminiscent of Magic Johnson. He couldn't shoot, but he could dunk. He helped us win many games.

Joey Wansack, from Sharon, Pennsylvania on the border of the Sandusky trail played good ball. We came over on the same plane. When he saw my name on the tryout list, he said he was going to try out too. He turned out to be a flat-out-knock-down shooter. We maintained a friendship for years.

One of our more competitive games we played into double overtime against Bitburg, and they were inferior to other teams we played. We should have beat them by at least twenty points, but we got full of ourselves. My guys had no bed check, so they'd pick up girls and stay out all night. Exceptional players, the guys thought they could walk on the floor, throw our name out there and make everyone bow. Bitburg reared their ugly heads and beat us bad the first half. We lost the game and I laid into those men. "Don't you ever step on the court half-ass. You always show up ready to battle." That game was over before it began. There are few things that I truly hate but hating to lose is at the top of the list. It's a sin to lose without a fight.

One of our biggest games was against an air force team in England. Chicksands had the winningest record three years running. It was an extremely competitive game and I went thirteen from fourteen from the field. Jump shots off the top of the key. Scored twenty-six points and never shot a foul shot.

There was a player called Ed Boxdale on the opposing team. He had height and size, was a power player, but he, like his teammates, was slow of foot. Against them, I instituted the Boston break: fast break, press them whole court, run up-tempo. Run, run, run. I made All- USAREUR with a 25.2 average. We won the championship and ended the season with a 62-5 record.

Baseball season was in full swing by July 4, 1962 when we played a double hitter in Nuremburg next to Soldier's Field. American track star Jesse Owens achieved international fame here, winning four gold medals at the 1936 Summer Olympics. Angelo Rosario, lead pitcher with the Stars and Stripes, hit a homerun, batting in two. As he ran the bases and rounded third, I took my left hand and patted him on his bottom. "Good job my boy," I said. When I looked up, snowflakes were falling from the sky. Can you imagine—snow in July? Back home family and friends sifted white sand through toes; I coached a baseball game in an inch of wintry white.

I inherited the baseball team and its 42-5 record. We put in hours of practice before the team turned around. An important five-game tournament was scheduled in scenic Nancy, France, a riverfront city known for old art nouveau and baroque markers. The winner flies to Fort Ord in California to play teams from Japan, Puerto Rico, and the states. If we hoist the championship trophy, the General's gain bragging rights.

My guys partied every day in the red-light district the month leading to my discharge. For two games they played mediocre at best, but enough to tie the series 2-2. Normally, I would have played, but I had already taken myself off the roster. I had also put another pitcher in the game, and it meant the world to him that he was given a chance to prove himself. I would not rob him of that feeling you get when you know you are standing on the threshold of greatness. If you've ever won a competition, even within yourself, then you know of the rush that pulses untamed through your body. You feel unconquerable.

He stepped into his moment and performed with all his heart. He did well. But he could not make up for the others who schlepped into the dugout hungover and lethargic. I let my team get away from me and we lost the European championship. It was a crushing defeat. We gave the win away. Either win by fighting hard or lose it fighting harder, but never, ever give a win away.

That was the last game of the season. It closed the door to two years of some of the most rewarding experiences of my young life. Next, it was time to walk through another door.

The General wanted me to enlist and travel with him as coach. What he really wanted was private golf lessons. Before I began basic training, they knew everything about me; including what hand I signed my name. They sent for my clubs before boot camp was even over: Wilson three wood, iron, and McGregor driver. I was instructing generals in the fundamentals of golf while other soldiers were sludging through the mud.

Golf was the easiest sport for me to teach but the hardest for anyone to learn. I've been a golfer all my life. Daddy taught me at ten years of age how to hit a ball. Ed Furgol, PGA pro, refined my skills and taught me why I'd hit the ball a certain way. Not only was I an outstanding golfer, I knew how to break down the game. It wasn't what I said, it was how I demonstrated the basics.

The air force bases had their own golf courses. We didn't play seaside golf, nor was it hilly. Snowmelt left the course green and lush, grasses framed the fairways. Ramstein had more trees and hazards, dense shrub, and deeper bunkers. It was laid out well. I represented the seventh army in stroke play. The person with the lowest score after four days won the tournament. If you win, the trophy goes into the unit's showcase. I had a 7-9 record.

I fought against the odds during those two brutal losses. The weather each tournament was cold, drizzly, and overcast. Leaves swirled from trees into the grey beyond. Sand traps were wet, heavy. Strangled, unforgiving rough swallowed balls left and right. In the states, I was accustomed to playing in tailor-made clothing: golf shirts, adjustable slacks, alpaca sweaters. Here I wore a heavy jacket and double socks. And still, it wasn't enough to get warm. My body couldn't adjust to the dropping temperatures. I could not keep my hands from tightening in the frigid air. I struck the ball like an eager first-time golfer who wants to do well but shanks the ball off the hosel 75-degrees to the right. My best that day was not the best needed to win. It was time to go home.

I discharged October 19, 1963 and went back to Riviera Beach one month before President John F. Kennedy was assassinated. I took incredible experiences with me including the army's seven core values, which I had all along, but the army helped me identify them. These are values worth having and sharing no matter your life's path:

Loyalty	Selfless Service	Personal
Duty	Honor	Courage
Respect	Integrity	

To thine own self be true. Before you can be loyal to anything or anyone, you must first be loyal to self. There is not one who will dispute my loyalty as a friend. I have battled beside those I am loyal to without judgment or regret. But I bear true faith and allegiance to God first.

There are no shortcuts in life. Duty obligates you to carry out tasks without expecting an effortless way out. It has been said "nothing good comes easy" but that is not true. When it comes easy to you, like sports has been for me, your duty then is to share your talents and strengths to help others along the way.

When Jackie Robinson spoke before a rapt audience of Roosevelt high schoolers, he said, "I don't care if you like me. All I ask is that you respect me." Treat people well. Period. The Ten Commandants advises us to "do unto others as you would have them do to you." Will you always be respected despite how you treat someone? Not always; but treat them well anyway. And sometimes that means walking away.

When you do something good for another and not look for praise or reward, you are selfless. The more you give, the more you get. Service is its own reward; satisfaction its payment.

Honor is the act of living out the other values. Enraged, suppose I had knocked my drill sergeant over the head. Not only would I have hurt him, but I would have dishonored the oath I took when I was drafted into the army. I would have dishonored myself and disgraced my family.

Integrity demands that you do what is right, not only when it is convenient, but especially when it is difficult. Do what you say you are going to do. Be a man or woman of your word. Whatever I tell you I will do you can believe I will see it through.

Personal courage is the basis of every value and it determines your path in life. It takes courage to follow your dreams despite the naysayers. Don't go to your grave wondering what if.

It takes courage to tell the truth when you're tempted to tell a lie. It requires courage to follow the rules when all your friends are breaking the law. It takes courage to say "No."

Mama told me, "Danny, don't you let nobody push you around." Stand up for yourself and others. Fight for the less fortunate.

Face your fears. Do what scares you the least so it will be easier to do what frightens you most. It's like training for a game. Practice. Practice. Practice. Courage is like a muscle. It must be conditioned, and massaged, and stroked.

Remember, when you are afraid, you give away your power. You can't win a game from the bench. Fear is an imaginary giant. It only exists in your mind. Be like David and slay it.

God has given you a spirit of courage. The Lord is your strength and is with you always.

I returned to Riviera Beach with the distinction of Manager of the Year. The generals presented me with an ornate plaque for my winning record with the Seventh Army Support Command. It was a great honor. Still unsure whether I'd return to Long Island, or if I'd go to school on the GI Bill. I thought I might even look for the man who had offered to put me through qualifying school to become a PGA member.

In 1962 integration paved the way for Blacks to play on public courses south of the Mason Dixon line. Many private courses remained segregated. We could work there but still not play during the day. For two years I worked and played beside some of the most tolerant, talented men I've ever known. If you're lucky, you have inspired experiences that disprove life's uglier truths. There are good people in the world who don't look like you; you can do what makes you happiest; you can live the life of your wildest dreams.

The 1996 Olympic Torch Relay

In Florida, the Olympic torch run started in Key West and upward to the Georgia line. Out of total 40,000 candidates, Palm Beach County had sixty-seven runners of 5,500 community heroes chosen. Torchbearers aged twelve or older could apply or be nominated in categories that included community heroes, Olympic athletes, and more.

The Riviera Beach city council nominated me as a community hero based on the Organizing Committee's criteria for defining a community hero. That included notable work as a volunteer, service as a community leader, role model, or mentor, acts of generosity or kindness, extraordinary feats, or accomplishments.

A welcome ceremony kicked off Olympic events on April 27, 1996. The Olympic flame landed at Los Angeles International Airport and began its eighty-four-day journey across the country. My group was briefed when the torch came from Miami. I started my leg on Day seventy-seven in Lantana, and, at fifty-eight years old, ran the entire distance through Lake Worth to West Palm Beach. This was my run and I was proud to represent the city and area where I was born and raised.

Mama, Faye, Nita, and Junior, few friends helped line the streets with chanting rhythms and inflections of pride. Delores jogged every inch alongside me. Mama tried to keep up. The local media covered the run and the festivities surrounding the event. I had a pinch me moment, surreal in its significance. You might live two hundred years and not meet another torch runner. And yet, here I stand, proud and free, unforgiving minutes filled with sixty seconds' worth of distance run.

When the torch reached the runners in Atlanta on July 19, thousands of cheering supporters greeted them. A one hundred-eighty footlong bridge linked Centennial Olympic Stadium to a metallic tower one hundred sixteen-feet-high, where a twenty-foot-high cauldron soon burned. Previously, the last torchbearer who crossed the bridge climbed the tower to the cauldron to light it. But, to make it easier for Muhammad Ali—whose identity until this day had been a secret—the flame travelled via a rope from inside the Stadium to the cauldron.

I have been blessed to do a lot of things. I place the Olympic torch run in the top of five.

Community Relations

I WAS ELECTED AS GRAND Marshal twice for the Martin Luther King Jr Parade. It was a high community honor. Banners with my name on the car's side fluttered in the breeze as I waved gratefully from the back seat.

As we crossed the very railroad tracks that kept them from us, I sat tall and proud atop the convertible's back seat. They announced from the grandstand: "Ladies and Gentlemen, our hero from S Avenue, Mr. Dan Calloway." For a moment, I allowed myself to bask in the glow of adoration. It felt good. A lifetime unbounded by formality. I honored those who came before me, and the ones who dare to follow. In spite of the day's pomp and circumstance, my greatest honor was yet unveiled.

I worked for the sheriff's office when they inaugurated the Dan Calloway Recreation Center. Sheriff Wille said, "This is the greatest honor anyone in the history of the Palm Beach Sheriff's Office has ever received. It couldn't go to a better person than Dan." Richard Wille stayed in office five terms without scandal or loss. I'd like to think I had something to do with his success on the job.

From the time I drafted plans for the gym with the architect, I could have never thought it would be anyplace other than the westside of the track. But it was built on the east side. There had to be something bigger than me at work.

An honor like none other, I was the first living person whose name graced an eight-million-dollar recreation facility replete with game rooms, classrooms, computer labs, and gyms theater.

The center means more to me than any of the more than three hundred awards and recognitions I've received over my lifetime. And still I rise.

When I started with the Sheriff's Office, I was head of the community relations unit. That was my job. I had a million-dollar budget covered the entire county. For me to keep the office looking good, I was out there every day. I went to different schools and talked about drugs, sexual assault, domestic violence. I wore plain clothes.

I wanted to make the police look like they cared about the community they served. I was allowed to be creative. Midnight basketball, Police Athletic League, parties with food and music. I was an expert speaker for National Black Social Workers convention. I talked about substance abuse, and drug trafficking, prostitution. Sadly, somewhere down the line the law took advantage of the people.

We influenced the drug dealers and gangs by getting them off the streets and in the courts late into the night. It was good to put the officers and thugs together. Police officers sees the thug as another human being. They'll get to know one another as ball players. Sport was the great equalizer. The men on the streets got to know the officers and crime went down significantly. Kids want to have something to do. Food brings them, music keeps them. The basketball games were the carrot dangled in their face. I'm still asked to put together programs for and leagues. I still feed thousands of people and serve gods children. This is God's prophecy, not mine. But I wouldn't do anything else.

A friend of Junior's was beating a woman with his fist outside on the main street of Riviera. Everybody standing around watching. "Rudy, stop hitting her."

He held her hair with one hand and just punched her face with his other. What man gets his kicks out of beating on a woman like that. He didn't stop so I jumped on him until he stopped. Then everyone else wanted to put their too cents in until I took a stance no one was thinking about helping this poor woman.

One of my classmates was beating his wife to the point of black eyes. She called me and said, "Your friend is over here beating on me." So, I went to his house to make sure she was well. Frank came home and asked, "What you are doing in my house talking to my wife?" He looked at me like who tied the bear.

"What you are doing hitting on your woman?" I defended her against her husband. He was bigger than me and nothing more than a quarter hustler. "You better not hit her again."

"What you think you gonna do?"

"You gonna answer to me."

I always defended the weak and the downtrodden and the helpless. I wasn't a bully, but I will never back down.

181

I mention these stories because Domestic Violence has always been an unspoken issue in the Black community. We must do better to address mental illness, anger management, and domestic abuse. Abuse is all about power and control. Everyone has the right to live free from abuse and harm. If you or someone you know is in an abusive relationship, call the national hotline number: 800-799-7233

Martin Luther King Jr. came to West Palm Beach in 1966. He and other civil rights activists had been traveling the south helping voter registration efforts. The meeting took place in the high school and the audience was full of the Vanguard of Black West Palm Beach. He spoke about us sticking together, how we can go much further together if we reach back and grab hold of our brother's hand. We've got to stick together. Every great people have come from an army. And they don't war with themselves. I am disappointed that we have yet to get that memo. Sixty years later we are no further along.

We are like crabs in a barrel. One day the barrel tipped over, the lid fell aside, and one self-seeking crab escaped. "Freedom!" shouted the crab. "What to do, what to do?" He looked around surveying the land. "Aah, so much to see and do." He noticed the lid of the barrel was out of place and a crab sitting at its edge. Instead of helping the others out he slammed the lid shut and walked away whistling. "I'm the king crab now."

That's how we are; king crabs wandering alone unwilling to abdicate the throne. We don't realize the throne and kingdom are not ours. We still have the slave mentality. We haven't broken the chains. We don't think of owning the business, we just want the paycheck working for someone else. We don't want the risk. Own the company. Put a couple dollars away each paycheck. Don't envy your brother. There's plenty to go around. Many don't get the chance.

In 1963 the 16th Street Baptist Church was bombed in an act of white supremacist terrorism, when four members of the Ku Klux Klan planted dynamite beneath the steps of the church. Four young girls were killed.

Freedom Riders, civil rights activists who rode buses into the segregated south 1961 and later years, challenged the non-enforcement segregated public bus systems. I stayed abreast of news with the Stars and Stripes, a newspaper that focused on topics concerning members of the United States Armed Forces. While I was overseas, the cares of the community seemed lightyears away. I was running the recreation department at the time. There aren't too many men who I consider an oratorical rival to Dr. King except Farrakhan.

When Farrakhan came years later, I was in his entourage. He had his own bodyguards and travel staff, but they were in my city and Sheriff Wille told me not to let things get out of hand. I don't get carried away by his ideology or militancy, but his message to the black community about self-sufficiency leaves much to reflect on.

For many years I volunteered as the athletic director for the Urban League as it coincided with my community relations duties out of the Sheriff's office. School, four-hours work, four hours in the sub-station, I sign off on the time so they could be paid. I took kids from low income projects to the Dolphin's games twice a year as part of the community relation initiatives.

I hold the parents responsible for a lot of the things wrong. Take off the rose-colored glasses. Whenever a parent says, "My child would never do that." That's a red flag. Your child is a child and always capable of doing something unthinkable. Never put your child in the position that makes him or her think that the law is for other people and not for you or him. I told a campus of kids one day, "We have fifty kids in this room. I can put five dollars on this desk and leave the room. I'll ask, 'where's my five dollars?' and no one will say who took it." That five dollars should never leave that desk. You know its not your money." If you don't have self-discipline you will be a loser. Nobody wins unless they have restraint. The rules and regulations must be enforced. You don't break the rules and you will never have to worry about going to jail. No one will ever have to yell at you. You are guilty by association if you remain silent.

All of life is good, bad, evil. We want to sugar coat everything, keep life from happening to our kids. Life is gonna throw you some curve balls. Human nature 101 demands movement. Flow with it. Idle hands are the devil's workshop. When you are weak it's easy to be influenced by peer pressure. Self-discipline leads to inner strength.

Most of the guys I grew up with snuck around smoking and drinking and doing things they shouldn't do; but I knew I wanted to be a professional athlete, so I wouldn't join them.

There's never a happy conclusion when you do something you know you shouldn't do. I don't know why, but Honeyman was attracted to trouble. Trouble found him even when he minded his own business. It was if a cloud followed him around all day.

Preacher Brooks had a pocketful of cash that Honeyman eyed all day. He was amused and began to fool around. Honeyman teased Preacher raw and impulsive, pushed up on him and took his money. Preacher stabbed Honeyman right above the kidney. Buck poured horse liniment on the wound. I told Mama Honeyman was bleeding and she rushed him to the hospital for stitches. Lord knows Mama was upset. Her poor child could have been killed. She took pride in four things:

1. Family
2. Church
3. School
4. Community

We took pride in ourselves. We were treated like second-hand citizens, and that gave me more incentive to do my best.

Bernard Gardner ran away from home for two or three days and nobody knew where he was. his mother came to the gym.

"Mr. Calloway, I can't find Bernard. He didn't come home, and we don't know where is."

A day later one of the kids told me where to find him. I found him and gave him a lecture. I said, "If you ever do that again I'm gonna beat you for ten minutes." Bernard was from a single-family home and was troubled during his teens. He turned out to be a great young man.

The NAACP worked out of the gym. The first race riot was in 1967. Three Black boys burned down the lumber yard. The timber was blazing high and wide. The Blue Heron bar was half block from the lumber yard and full of people. White people were upset because Mullins Lumber was burning down to the ground. Mr. Mullins lumber yard was gone. He employed a lot of people in town and owned many of the homes we rented. Everybody started gathering around. Tensions were rising.

"Y'all go on home." I said. "Go home now."

The adults disappeared inside the Blue Heron and the children walked west lamenting injustices.

Segregation was passed. Riviera High turned into Suncoast High and Kennedy became a junior high school. In February, Claude Brown asked his teacher, "When are we going to talk about Black History like we normally do this month?"

His teacher, recently transferred under the new law, "We not going to worry about no niggers."

He walked up to the desk and cussed her out. She reported the matter to the dean, and he expelled Claude. By now news had spread from one classroom to the next and before you know it the whole school spilled into the hallways. The dean called the police, the police came and threw tear gas into the screaming crowd. Everyone scattered crying, yelling, and throwing rocks. One in the children flagged me down and we hurried over to the school. The chief ran up to me and said, "Danny, you got to help us."

"No, you done messed up. You had no business teargassing them."

The Palm Beach County Sheriff descended upon the area with forty officers, tear gas and Billy clubs in hand yelling, "Y'all dispense. Dispense."

We told the children not to move. They hadn't done anything wrong. I went to the Sheriff. "Give me five minutes."

I got a few of the big boys, "Tell all those kids clear this parking lot and come to the gym at 7:00." That's all I said, and they showed up at the gym. Over a thousand people showed up at the gym. Two months later we fired the police chief, added three black council members, and the complexion of the city changed.

We changed the government. We had one Black councilman. We retained control of the city since then. When there is dissention in the ranks and complaining, we can't blame it on whites.

In our town when we couldn't be on the eastside of the tracks after seven o'clock, when we couldn't go to the same hospital and schools, we finally got the power. The principal resigned. The teacher transferred. The students went back to learning. Never no more will you treat us like secondhand citizens.

Tracy Martin was an excellent baseball player. He played league ball for a Miami team and another one called" I-95 south" that played against our team. The prime minister of Nassau asked if I'd participate in a co-ed softball tournament. I agreed although I no longer had my male team, only the ladies. Tracy agreed to play and bring a few guys, but he need a favor. He had to bring Trayvon. "I promised my boy. I need him to come."

I had a strict rule no children could travel with the team, but I gave in or I'd lose my star player. Trayvon was in sixth grade and stayed with me and Clark while the guys were on the field. For three days he stuck with us like glue. Extremely kind and well-mannered, he said "yes sir, no sir, thank you, please."

Seven years passed and a boy grew into a young man. And still, parents do what they must do. Tracy brought his boys whenever he played in tournaments. He said publicly that I had been like a daddy. "He has been like a father for the last ten years."

Althea and Gail came up to me one day and asked if I had heard the news. It was Trayvon. Tracy's son gunned down in a senseless killing. His killer thought his life was in danger and stood his ground against a boy with no weapon walking home. I commend Tracy and Sybrina. They displayed a courage and grace under fire that I pray few will have to know. Gracious in their interviews, articulate in their communication with the press and media. I hope to never know the pain of what they have experienced. My sons and grandsons are Black men in a trigger-happy America. But the bullets are flying from every direction.

Mother's Against Murderers Associated works to bring a modicum of solace and support to mothers who have lost children to senseless acts of violence. MAMA started fifteen years ago after two sisters lost three boys within three months, victims of drug violence in our community. Since its inception, the mothers associated with MAMA have buried over four hundred sons and daughters as a direct result of gun violence.

No one should fear walking home day or night or getting pulled over by the law. As a retired Palm Beach County detective, I share a few things you can do to protect yourself, though there will always be good cops/bad cops; just as there will always be good citizens/bad people.

Citizens

1. Most officers are good
2. Follow the rules and obey the law
3. Keep hands in view at all times when approached by an armed officer. Cops keep eyes on your hands
4. The bad police officer is waiting for you to say something confrontational or get you to act violent. You take your life into your hands if you do.
5. The dashcam and bodycam is your friend. It is the best thing that ever happened for Black people
6. No one should ever shoot at a police officer.
7. Do exactly what the officer says. Even if they are wrong, do exactly what they say
8. A male officer should never search a female suspect without a female officer present

Police

1. Remember most police officers have the ability to process things fairly and quickly
2. Every department has SOPs that should be updated regularly.
3. There must be better training in-house every three months.
4. A good police officer should never leave his or her car without a backup.
5. Even if it's a traffic stop, call for back up.

6. Reevaluate why you stopped a driver. Some stops are unnecessary.

7. Run the tag before you get out the car. If the tag isn't clear use your microphone to ask them to step out the car, hands away from the body.

PBC Sherriff's Department

THE RIVIERA BEACH POLICE chief came from the Federal Bureau of Investigation. He told us J. Edgar Hoover was his hero because he was head of the FBI in the same way Martin Luther King Jr. was our hero because he was the face of the civil rights movement. This Black man had to be the worst person in the world. He worked for the city and tried to destroy anyone who had a modicum of power or standing in the community.

I didn't want it to appear as if I was jealous of a man who headed a department which I had been offered to run, in a city in which I was reared. I could have never been an officer in Riviera Beach. I knew all the hot spots, where things used to be done, where things were being done, and the people breaking the law. I had to live up to the code.

Because of my position in community, elected officials and I have always butted heads. I will not make anyone feel like they are the greatest thing since sliced bread. That doesn't bode well with bureaucrats who expect to be placated. I will never cheapen me; I will never go along to get along. If I ruffle feathers so be it.

Some time back, I was in a meeting discussing the governor's race. A city administrator said, "I saw you in the media recently. When you spoke, everybody cringed because they didn't know if you were about to call them to the carpet."

See, I am a wide-open book, black or white, never grey. If I have something to say, I speak; if I don't, I stay quiet. When I talk, you get the truth whether it sits well with you or not. When I can avoid trouble, I do. Push comes to shove; I say what I believe is true. I must sleep with, wake to, and look at Dan Calloway in the mirror and like what stares back at me. I care little to none whether you feel good about me; I must feel good about myself, even when I'm tested.

My friend Al was always the brother from another mother. He and I grew up playing stickball and football with Burt Reynolds in the streets east of the tracks. Conchtown was an area settled by Bahamian immigrants in the early nineteen hundred. To claim yourself "Conch" in Key West was a symbol of pride, but Riviera "Conch" was used similar to the N-word to disparage mixed-race Bahamians. They passed as White and took offense to the name.

We were children interested only in bats, balls, and Bazooka bubble gum. We didn't care if you were purple with a horn growing from the middle of your head; all we wanted was to play a competitive baseball game. Despite our differences, Al and I became fast friends. We played side by side with the White kids during the day. The local people never bothered us as long as we stood on the westside of the FEC railway tracks by 7:00 p.m., one of many Jim Crow laws that, if you broke you, you paid the piper. You must return to "colored town" before dusk.

Al ran the fish markets and marina shops in the area. When I was with the Recreation Department, he supplied hundreds of pounds of fish for community events we sponsored. We became business partners and built a profitable shop, carrying goods like bait, tackle, food, beer, and wine. Law enforcement employees cannot profit from the sale of alcohol, so I leased the business to Al and his wife, and they paid me rent.

I also owned a laundromat where Al oversaw operations and submitted monthly receipts to me. Months later he got in trouble selling drugs in Alabama. When he returned to Riviera Beach, he promised never to get involved in drugs or illegal activity again. I believed him. I will take your word too until you prove to me that I can't trust you. I had no reason not to trust him.

Dockmaster, Al allowed boats to come in without oversight. Lots of contraband found its way in. A guy from Pittsburg who I didn't know wanted to buy my share of the store to use as storage for drugs. I was clueless about any wrongdoings.

Some say I am loyal to a fault, but I trusted Al and saw no reason to not believe him. We were like brothers. For crying out loud, we drank from the same soda bottles. I ate lobster at his table every week.

When Al got arrested the police chief tried to brand me guilty by association. A lieutenant asked me to sever my relationship with Al and disclose what I knew about his operations. Everyone, including the sheriff, knew I would not get involved in criminal activity. I love my family far too much to bring shame on them this way.

A few years before this incident, there was a Federal grand jury investigation of organized crime in the area. They targeted powerful Blacks, looking for complicity. The FBI made their case, but I guess they weren't satisfied. Doesn't matter. I will always tell the truth because I have always been on the right side of the law. I stood before the news media and told them, "Al is my friend. I will not forsake him now. He is my friend with a wife and two kids." I did not abandon him.

My business was confiscated in 1992. I walked away with eighteen thousand dollars though it was worth close to a quarter million. I paid the lawyer fees and signed the remainder over to Al's wife because the city took their house. The police chief and city manager worked together and fired three employees then came for me. Since I wasn't a municipal employee nothing could be done. But we decided to sue to reclaim my business.

My attorney said, "We got em."

Riviera Beach had a mayor and city manager. Five of six council members were black. Personal friends cast three out of five votes. One was Bucky McGann. I didn't want anyone to say Bucky voted for me out of a sense of loyalty to his friend. I couldn't put him in that position. I forfeited the two hundred fifty thousand dollars.

Al spent eight years in jail. He said the reason he didn't tell me about his other life was because he knew I would have been mad. A weak excuse but he owned up to it. Once again, I believed him, as the urge to knock him over the head loomed large. He had given me his word this time would be different, and I never questioned him.

Gambler, drunk, a liar, friend. If I had to do it over again, I would, without batting an eye. Everyone makes mistakes. Some slip-ups bite harder than others, but the cure is the same: forgiveness. He needed a second chance. I stayed his friend until we buried him in 2016. I was the only Black person in the church. With the money I gave her, his wife bought a trailer in Alabama beneath a grove of longleaf pines.

My foray into the world of politics and law happened by chance. The Urban League director Percy Lee asked would I talk to Richard Wille, the man challenging William Heidtman for sheriff of Palm Beach County. I wanted to put it off, but Percy convinced me to give him a few minutes of my time. "He's not gonna win anyway," he told me. "Bill is a powerful man. No way is he going to lose."

Richard and I agreed to meet at my fish market, which was in a little strip plaza near Herman McCray's restaurant. In 1974 I opened Calloway Fish Market with Lamar Parrish. He bailed out, even though the business was popular and profitable. My suppliers, who were white, began overpricing fish and sundries and underselling to my competitors. I was undercut at every turn, but we kept turning a profit, and the suppliers kept raising prices. Eventually I had to pass on the increase to my customers.

Straight to the point I said, "Richard. If you become Sheriff with barely six hundred employees, eighteen blacks, four sworn officers, fifteen in the jail, you gonna have to change that. If it wasn't so sad it would be embarrassing." Palm Beach was one of the largest and wealthiest counties in the country yet far removed from the concerns of the working class.

"That's one of the first things I will address," Richard said.

We needed Blacks in personnel and administrative positions. We needed more Blacks in the jails. The department needed an overhaul to reflect the changing landscape of the county. Boone Darden, Riviera's first Black police chief, and Lopez, a Hispanic who identified as white, also announced their run for sheriff. I liked what Richard was saying so I shut my fish market down and I threw my hat in the ring. Turned out to be one of the best decisions I've ever made.

I didn't believe in fighting dirty, pitting one against the other with insults and innuendo. I was out canvassing and stopped at a Jewish community center where Lopez heartily campaigned as an incumbent. He spoke disparagingly against Boone, one of the highest-ranking Black officers in the south. Lopez, who didn't know I was in the room, spouted a host of lies to sell his position. Then, he lowered the gauntlet.

"Would Y'all rather have a nigger in there to tell you what to do or someone who looks like you?"

Well, that was all the ammunition I needed. I stood before the group black as the pit and gave them without slander or deceit every good reason to vote for Sheriff Wille. They offered their support for Richard and voted for him in the primaries. I used this incident to

All the while, I'm telling Richard what he should and shouldn't be doing once he gets in office. I knew what we needed to keep kids off the street, how to garner support from the community, how to use the office to make a difference. He got so tired of hearing my mouth he pulled me aside and said, "Stop telling me what to do; join me and help me do it."

The rest is history. Boone lost against Lopez in the primaries and Wille defeated Heidtman with little to spare. On January 4, 1977 Richard Wille became sheriff and I became the fifth Black sworn officer in the history of Palm Beach County Sherriff's Office. Ten weeks at the academy, I received with pride my law enforcement certification and became the chief's troubleshooter.

My main job was to stop gang violence, prevent riots, sniff out the bad and keep it from happening. How I'd accomplish that for some seemed a monumental feat. I welcomed the challenge open-armed. I didn't wear a uniform which made it easier to relate to people on the streets. I went to all the schools and lectured on the perils of substance abuse and crime. I took fourth graders to professional games and training camps.

After we established the community relations department, I spoke at various political functions and social events, traveled countrywide and spoke at colleges, universities, and police departments. I hired men and women considered unemployable by departments in other cities. The autonomy afforded to me was unprecedented.

One day I met with Richard and the states attorney and said, "Gather the police chiefs and start a league. It's good for public relations. Kids will come, police officers will coach. The department will benefit from the increased visibility in the community." Soon after, I brought the Police Athletic League to Palm Beach County. We established a national league so our teams could travel the country. But we needed money, so I wrote grants, solicitation letters and requests for funds. I was invited to pitch US Sugar.

The western part of Palm Beach County was all farmland and vegetation owned by US Sugar. Four senior officers and I flew by helicopter to meet with company executives. The group, comprised of a colonel, captain, and two lieutenants, got upset when they learned I was to present. Does this mouthy black man, two years on the job, really think he can speak for us? They didn't like me anyhow and that just stoked the flames. Whatever I did, they fought tooth and nail. I didn't sit around and joke with them. I refused to play the dozen. Don't tell me to do something, come and do it with me. That is how I conducted myself.

We arrived and entered an imposing conference room with portraits of company executives staring at us from the walls. An impressive mahogany table filled the room. After an introduction of parties, I extolled the virtues of the company, their economic impact in the county, and such. But then I told them what I was really trying to do.

"The PAL will help us stop gang violence, decrease crime, enable kids to go to college," I said. "We have budgeted one million dollars and need your help."

They asked, "So what are you asking from us?"

"I am asking for you to put up the first two hundred fifty thousand dollars. When you do, others will follow suit, and you will forever be known as the company who first supported such an important endeavor."

My colleagues nearly fell out their seats when they heard how much money I sought. Heads on the desk, digging a whole in the floor, it was clear they thought I ruined any chance of getting a dime. How dare I ask for that amount of money? Fifty, sixty thousand maybe, but a quarter million dollars? They were fuming and didn't hide it.

"Gentlemen, please give us a moment." The executives disappeared around the corner. It felt like an hour had passed yet the conference room felt eerily calm. Ten minutes later they returned looking somber and resolute. We didn't know what to expect. "Well Sargent since you had the nerve to ask, we're pleased to help."

My colleagues danced on the ceilings they were so happy. When we got back into the copter, I laid into them. "I ought to shove all Y'all outside this plane and fly it back myself."

Once the League got up and running, we started to see a small decrease in crime. There will always be an element of criminality regardless of the relationship between citizen and police. A gun makes these boys feel invincible. So many are fatherless, dead, or incarcerated. When a one hundred forty-pound boy has a pistol in his head, you can put three two hundred-pound men in front of him and he won't flinch.

For that reason, I didn't carry a weapon. In the beginning I kept it concealed. I did a lot of lecturing and asked my audiences, are you respecting me because I have a revolver in my holster or because I'm a police officer? My colleagues were always fearful for me. But I had no fear. I was the Major league player turned cop. Every town made my job easier. I sent kids to college. The gun is part of your uniform. You had to qualify with your weapon every year, but because I had vertigo, I was relieved of carrying. Because I was gun-less, I was able to maintain better relations. My greatest weapon was my ability to talk. It took me years to reach this point but when I arrived, I stayed.

I didn't have a chain of command. I reported to Sheriff Wille and the undersheriff. My job was toughest because I was working directly at the whims of the sheriff. The ranking officers resented it. I came to work when I came to work. I might have to be out at night. I had carte blanche.

My biggest accomplishment on the force was having no riots. I put together programs at all the games. The schools were integrated in 1972. I went to away games with the teams. I spent time in the schools. Before school board security the police did the school security. I'd assign officers to the schools. They were given the latitude to do their jobs. We'd eat lunch with the kids, organize assemblies, and kept order. No one went against the green and white. Except the green and white.

Every time a job opened, I recruited at the Black colleges. We need more diversity in the ranks. Sometimes minor infractions kept men and women off the force. I was on the force 1977 - 2002 and I recruited over two hundred officers. When I retired there might have been over nine hundred Black officers in the department. Richard Wille credits me for saving his career.

One of the most disappointing aspects of the job for me is the racism is still rampant. Law enforcement is a White man's job. It is the only job where you have license to kill someone. I was treated bad when I first began. I had letters put in my box. The Sheriff was a fair man. He set the bar high for any white.

We had a Haitian inmate who died in custody because no one could understand him when he got sick. He spoke in Patois and went misunderstood his entire stay. The city was liable and had to pay the family a million dollars. He didn't want to hear about any racism. The SOP was changed so there would be at least one translator of a non-English speaking inmate at all times.

I brought tuition reimbursement to the department. I got my certifications. I was Sheriff Wille's troubleshooter. I brought the junior deputy program. We distributed turkeys and Christmas baskets every year. It was a big program that continues to this day. They went to people in need no matter the race or creed. When the county fair came in January and I get free tickets for the families in the communities. We brought busloads of kids to the Atlanta Braves training camps. There were many things we did that made a difference in the community for black and white alike. There is still so much more to do.

Interracial relationships were looked upon with jaundiced eyes during the segregation. Law enforcement is a white man's job, and the promotion was we didn't Internal affairs was investigating. I've been upset. Nat was a captain up for promotion. He was dating the unit secretary. The man doing the background check to was wrong. That's got to stop. The promotion was a terrible thing. He deserved to be a captain. I was on them about that. I stood up for him after he asked me if I burn the bridge, I might not be able to. One incident is not going to stop movement. I went to law enforcement to make a difference.

THE COACH

Sports Attributes

Most good coaches have the mental ability to see the weaknesses of their opponents as well as the strengths of his team. If the best shooter is right-handed, the only way he will dribble the ball and go toward the basket, he's going for his right, dominant hand. I will pick that up and tell the player on to take his right hand away, play on the right side, make him go to the left. What you are doing is making him take his second best to beat your first best.

In warmups you check out the athletes, how they shoot, how they walk, their nerves. If they are hyper and nervous, stay on top of them. Watch the first step, how the ball comes off their hands. A lot of coaches in the beginning stages do nothing more than yell. You've got to be observant and practice. Some of the best coaches are sticklers for detail. They taught the fundamentals and called the plays.

Take basketball. A coach might start with a man to man defense, and all at once he sees two guys that can really drive the ball to the basket. To keep the opponent from putting up a basket he has to put up a zone. Make him shoot from outside. Until he starts to knock down outside shots, you just keep him out there. Most kids who are great at an early age are going to the basket. It's much harder to make a basket from fifteen feet out than laying it up on the glass.

Its always easier to teach natural talent. A basketball player with natural talent can jump, and everything is reflex and hand-eye-coordination. Only people that can play basketball well are naturally talented.

To play baseball you don't have to be talented you just have to be smart. Once you learn the fundamentals, you'll be strong if you work at it.

Look at football. You just need to know the game well and be intimidating. An aggressive little man will always beat a scared big man.

But basketball, you've got to have talent. When everything is so quick, talent is the only thing that can keep up.

Once you learn to break the game down, you'll became dangerous. To be good, you must learn to recognize potential; recapitulate everything. When you picture what the opponent will do before he does it, you eliminate all the things he's not going to do, and it gives you one or two things that he can do. And that goes for anything in life. Know who you're up against.

Instinct

Talent you are born with, God has given it to you. You can take a kid with the least amount of ability and teach him or her the fundamentals of the game and turn her into an all-star. Talent makes a person adjust in a split second.

A talented person with instinct can make a mistake look like its part of the play. Instinct can't be taught.

If I'm playing baseball and the ball is hit in the right center field, I don't need the third base coach to motion to me to get to third base. I will peep over my right shoulder, see the ball in between the right fielder and centerfielder and in a split second can tell if the ball will get all the way to the wall. I have to veer out to the right off second base, make the loop to hit third base inside to make it home.

See, the coach didn't teach me that. That was something I instinctively knew and honed as a ten-year-old; That's talent. It's preordained. Whatever the play, I have to prepare as if it's coming to me and I'll react to it when it comes. When the ball is hit, all eight on the field move.

If I'm playing football and a man is running from the side, I rely on my split and peripheral vision, out the corner of my eye, if I can see the man coming on my left I will either veer to my right or stop abruptly and cut back to my left to dodge him up. Nobody can teach that. You have to have that true of instinct. Some of the best runners of all time can't tell you how they did it. Instinct tells you when to move and when not to move.

Imagine Lebron has the ball, starts moving toward the basket, and out of his eye he sees a man in the left corner open. He'll look to his right so everyone will think he's about to throw it to his right, he'll throw a blind pass to the left. Split second reaction.

Not everyone can react that quickly, but that's what sets the greatest apart from the good. Instinct comes before it even happens. You know if it does this, then you must do that. Instantaneously. The greatest athletes rely on instinct.

Technique

Technique makes you a well-rounded player. That's why I studied the fundamentals and read as many books I could get. Only at a certain level, a talented person in basketball always has the advantage. Basketball is eighty to ninety percent instinct. The best players do acrobats in the air and they don't even know that they're doing it. Technique is learning, practicing, and applying fundamentals. Many people have raw talent. Talent allows you to learn the fundamentals easier.

I thought I knew how to play golf well until I met professional golfer Ed Furgol. I was playing well but didn't know why. Technique teaches you the why and how. Talent pairs well with technique.

Take my softball player. I don't care if they're talented. I want to see that they're not scared and that they'll stick with it. No one can hit for you. Although you are playing as a team, each move is an individual move. No one can hit for the hitter but the hitter, but the pressure starts with pitcher. The pitcher has to get the ball over the plate. He has to get it over the plate where the batter doesn't knock it out the ballpark. Keep less power off the ball. He doesn't have to strike out everyone, but he has to be smart. In business, the closer you are to those you manage, the better off.

Athleticism

You cannot beat a person with a lot of athletic ability and talent. It won't happen. All he or she has to do is not be crazy and arrogant. Conceit will eventually bring you to ruin. What a person lacks in size, he can make up for with athleticism. If you put together two people of equal talent and ability, the more athletic of the two will win, every time. But athleticism must be honed like talent. Talent is not a learned behavior, but like athleticism, can be practiced and strengthened.

Work Ethic

I had an athlete who was a baseball junkie. Every day after school he wanted me to practice with him. He would keep me out there as long as he could just hitting popups. Red dog was small and good. You couldn't get the ball by him. I hit a lot of balls to him. But he didn't have a good bat. But because of his work ethic he got better. When I trained for the pros, I ate, slept, and drank baseball. I went to sleep dreaming about it and awoke with it on my mind. I played sandlot ball after school and didn't neglect my homework or chores. When I learned golf, I practiced my swings, chips, and putts, every day. Work for your dream.

Imagery

Every great athlete sees the play before it ever materializes. There is nothing made that wasn't born in a person's mind. I was born with natural athletic ability, but I saw myself playing with Jackie Robinson and remember every move I learned watching pros at the training field. My talent was a gift. But I laid in my bed every night envisioning a future as a professional baseball player. How is it then that my dreams came true?

Attitude

When you have a defeatist attitude, you've lost before the game ever starts. But when you believe you are going to win while staying within the framework of the rules, you have the advantage. You can take your opponent's nerve. Muhammad Ali told us he was "The Greatest." He once said, "If you even dream of beating me you better wake up and apologize." That's some kind of attitude. Whether cockiness or self-assuredness, it's all attitude and it separates the good from the best.

When I lost the spelling bee in the fifth grade, I was a sore loser. I hated to lose. I think I hated to lose more than I loved to win. Mama got so upset with me for pouting that she threatened to pull me off the teams. A bad attitude can be divisive, unloving, and detrimental to your performance. Whereas your body responds positively when your attitude is upbeat and fair.

Sportsmanship is critical if you want to go far. No one likes a bad sport.

I introduced Lawrence Taylor at a big tournament at Trump International Golf Club in West Palm Beach. We hosted a lot of celebrities, athletes, and public figures. We raised funds for the

Youth Recreation Association. Everyone was gathered around for the pretournament festivities when I took to the podium.

"He didn't play well, but one of my favorite linebackers and one of the best who's ever played, number 56 Lawrence Taylor."

Lawrence jumped up and said, "Ugh, Mr. Calloway, you're going too far. I'm not one of the best; I am the best!"

That's attitude.

Execution

Every year I had to paint the house. Every week I had to cut the lawn. If anything was left to be desired, I'd have to do it again. Daddy told us, "Do it right and you won't have to do it over."

My kids were required to take ten laps around the ballpark then I'd look like I wasn't paying attention. They'd cut across the field, unaware I had watched through a pair of binoculars every move.

Martin Luther King Jr. said, "If you can't fly then run, if you can't run then walk, if you can't walk then crawl, but whatever you do you have to keep moving forward."

I expected my athletes to keep moving, to never give up or give in, on or off the playing field. Like a job well done, executing the play skillfully is its own reward. Learn the fundamentals, practice, repeat.

Slave mentality

Daddy wasn't afraid of anyone, but he didn't want to lose a job. He called the younger men "Mister" and he said "Yessir" to everyone. When I became a man, I asked him, "Daddy, why do you do that?"

He was called the N-word often. I thought to myself, there is no way in the world I was going to let any man talk to me in a demeaning way. I had no fear. Nothing made me afraid to protect my family or friends.

The caddies at the end of the year got merchandise and twenty-five dollars for shooting the best score. I was never afraid to hold a conversation with members. I never found it hard to talk to white or wealthy people. I took it upon myself to ask the members to supplement anything the caddies needed. Never look down. I don't assume that tomorrow will get here, I have to earn my wings every day. "Blood sweat and tears kill a mosquito with a hammer."

Adversity

Don't have a safety pin mentality. When I as a boy with three brothers ahead of me, I always had hand me downs three deeps. Mama had a box of safety pins. When buttons came off my shirt, she had Gene take a pin out the box and fasten my shirt. When she'd get home, I'll sew on a new button with her. A safety pin is a temporary fix, not a permanent one. It's like adversity—this too will pass.

The best way to handle adversity is to never let a person see you sweat. My strength has always been to be able to outsmart and outthink others when they thought I was going to be country dumb. I relied on my intellect and cunningness over my talent. Adversity comes all the time. When my professional baseball career ended abruptly, I made lemonade from lemons and started a new chapter.

Integrity

Don't tell a lie. Always tell the truth. If you do a job right, you will always have a job. Mama told us about a rainy day. I wasn't going to let daddy kill hold anything over my head. My brother cooked dinner and junior would give me the back and feet and neck. If I complained, they would lie and say I had a bigger piece. Then I 'd hold onto something they did and use it against them when it was convenient. That was dishonest. But it made me feel better when they picked on me. Saving a lie to suit myself. Don't lie, tell the truth, stand up for what is right.

Riviera Beach Recreation Dept

I LEFT NEW YORK IN the midst of the Harlem Riots that began after James Powell was shot and killed by a police officer in front of his friends. President Kennedy was assassinated. Riots flared up everywhere. Martin Luther King marched. Stokely Carmichael and the Black Panthers raised hell. People plundered, pillaged, and ran from stores with hams and TVs, cutting up like fools. I will never understand how people justify vandalizing businesses owned by folks who have nothing to do with them. What does it profit a man to burn down his neighbor's house?

Two miles from my New York apartment was Shea Stadium and the World's Fair. Mama travelled from Florida to Connecticut to visit with her grandchildren. While she was up north, I promised to take her to the fair.

"Gene will put you on the New Haven Line and I'll pick you up at Grand Central Station," I told her. "You'll stay with me for four days."

When Mama stepped onto the Flushing Meadow fairgrounds she was like an overjoyed schoolgirl with new shoes. A stainless steel Unisphere towered one hundred forty feet high. Flags from every nation waved in the cool northern winds. People of every race, creed, and gender sat side by side at the reflecting pool. Others strolled about in native garb.

The Fair's theme was "peace through understanding." Paradoxically, a satirical minstrel show, staged at one of the pavilions, triggered protests by the NAACP who believed the show was demeaning to Blacks. They didn't want us to cross the picket line and patronize the expo.

I took Mama's hand and we crossed the line. We spent all day at the fair and had a beautiful time. Full circle moments happen when least expected. I was reminded of Mama's refusal to work after giving us her word she'd be with us for the Holiday. We were so happy to have our mother home. I was not going to disappoint her.

Home from Germany three months, I had to figure out what to do with my life. First things first, return to Riviera Beach. Faye begged me to go back to school on the GI bill. At the time it didn't fit the bill. In my mind, I was still a professional athlete, evidenced by my experiences overseas.

I hadn't been home two days when Captain Albert Henry Davis of the Riviera Police Department approached me to join the Force. I told him definitively years before I would never be a police officer. I knew where everybody shot dice, played cards, and gambled. Nope, not gonna do it.

"Well, you know we've wanted you for Recreation Director," he said.

This made sense to me. God doles out talents to us all. It's what we do with our gifts despite leaky roofs that determines the course our lives take. I always felt God had given me an overabundance of ability; now I must be a good steward of those talents. To whom much is given, much is expected. Now is the time to decide: hindrance or help? I accepted the call.

December 1964, I started working at the outdoor Goodmark Park. A sign read, "Welcome our new director, Dan Calloway." I was hired as the recreation supervisor and within four months was named assistant director. It was a natural fit because I was born an athlete. Growing up, my life was about fun and games.

Goodmark park was the mecca of everything before Tate gym opened. Royal palm and mango bordered the northside of the park. Inside the fenced perimeter kids twirled dizzily on the merry-go-round, boys and girls teetered on seesaws and jumped off swings without reserve. Adolescents shot net-less hoops.

Inside the building was my first office. Whatever door you walked through, there was my gray metal desk in plain view. To the right a ping-pong table, two card tables just beyond. A safe space where kids played, ate, studied, and dreamed.

Unrivaled was the joy of teaching kids who couldn't walk and chew bubble gum at the same time. Everyone who came through those doors was given a chance to play on a team or do a job. My assistant, Johnny Carlisle, a polio survivor and paraplegic, was one of those individuals.

Johnny played a mean game of ping pong. Daily he showed up, wide smile plastered across his face, greeted everyone in his path, and headed for the table. He was able to use his upper body in a way to lean against the table in a superhuman-like way. He outplayed the most skilled opponent. I recognized his talent and coached him to a gold medal for ping pong at the Paralympics.

As a coach, that was my greatest moment. The look of pride on Johnny's face when they draped a gold medal around his neck was a moment I'll never forget. And he was one of many who, in my eyes, stood tall among giants. Daily, hundreds of men and women with disability greeted me with sparkling eyes and warm hellos. I had always seen them as nothing more than smiling faces in broken bodies incapable of competing at a championship level in any sport, much less twenty. My perspective was forever altered that day after I witnessed God's hand upon those gifted athletes. I have not looked at a person with disability the same since.

Johnny didn't want to be treated differently. He couldn't run up and down the court, but I knew he could coach the kids and shoot foul shots with them. He was with me long enough to pay his way through college and earn a master's degree. He taught school for over thirty years.

In 1966, two years after I joined the recreation department, I sat at my desk and watched kids storm the door as the sky emptied in torrents. South Florida's humid subtropical climate delivers heavy unexpected bursts of rain in the heat of the day. The rainy season, May through September, finds children out of school and in need of safe, supervised spaces. We needed an indoor gym. The next day, I drafted plans for one similar to Eastern Parkway Arena in Brooklyn. That was the only indoor gym I'd seen with a boxing arena and was open to the public around the clock.

The plan was presented to the city council and unanimously approved. After fourteen months, we cut ribbon for Tate gym, named after the first Black Palm Beach County casualty of the Korea War. We were the first in the county with a city-run indoor gym. The building had a basketball court with bleachers, three game rooms attached to the gym that housed pool tables, ping-pong tables, a boxing ring, and kitchen.

After the successful opening of Tate, there grumbled in the east voices of dissent. "We can't send our children over there." So, the council approved a second gym. They broke ground for Well's Recreation, which was named for a councilman and icehouse owner. One director of recreation, one athletic director, and one center director ran the facilities.

Some of the greatest athletes who have ever played have gone through our doors. It became the gathering place for community events and tournaments. I had the ability to teach, coach, and organize any sport for the benefit of community in the city.

It was here that an umber-skinned runt with toothless smile played biddy basketball, firmly imprinting himself in my eyes as one of the top three all-around athletes ever. A bright-eyed seven-year-old, Anthony Carter played league basketball with unmatched instinct. He was a monster: fast, strong, and nimble with the best hand eye coordination of any athlete. With unparalleled foot speed, his talent was undeniable. Over the years he readily participated in programs associated with an evolving recreation department. In high school, he played football for Coach Sutton. Before that, he had to go through me.

Anthony outclassed his peers in little league baseball. An outstanding twelve-year-old centerfielder, he easily could have had a pro baseball career. One game, I was walking the field; he was in the dugout as required. His girlfriend strolled up to the fence, stuck her thin hand through the wire links and playfully tugged at his hair. "Leave me alone," he said. Bothered, she did it again.

"Goddammit! I told you to leave me alone!" Anthony yelled.

He didn't know I stood ten yards behind him but everyone on the field saw me and at full volume chanted, "Uh-oh. Uh-oh." Somebody's in trouble when you hear that chant. He turned around and found me looking at him square in the eyes.

"Come here boy," I said. "What did you say?"

"I didn't say nothing," he said, telling a snot-nosed lie.

I was a recreation director making and enforcing rules long before I was paid for the job. That's when me and cussing got our start. Mama didn't swear unless she was swearing to God. "I swear before God if I ever hear you using profanity, I'll wash your mouth out with Life Buoy." She didn't have to tell me twice. At sixteen, little boys begged me to play ball with them. If I heard them cussing, which I did, I'd cut a switch and tear their legs up. And send them home too. I didn't curse in front of them, they better not raise sand and cuss in front of me.

Mama couldn't attend baseball games during the day, so Buck brought her and Faye to see me play basketball at night. There was a campus shop in front of the high school where kids hung after the game. A lot of the older boys shot dice in front betting and cussing like sailors. Mama and Faye waited outdoors for her ride home in earshot to the campus shop. Those kids knew to tone it down whenever near the loves of my life.

"Y'all better not cuss and fuss in front of his sister and mama because he'll come over here and beat you up."

They knew in front of Faye they better act like a gentleman, and they threw that in my face all the time. "You quick to put up a bridge around your sister and yet you are doing whatever you want to everybody else's sister." That was true, but I wasn't out there cussing and fussing. I was very protective of Faye. You are going to respect my sister. What you do for your sister is up to you. Mama told us we better always take care of our sister. Daddy told us "I might get mad and fuss with your Mama, but you better always protect her. She will always be there even if I walk away." Those were non-negotiable rules in our house.

Anthony knew of the no cussing policy. Had he admitted his wrong, there'd be no problem. At most, I would have made him do laps and sit out the rest of the game. I told him, "First you apologize to your little girlfriend." I was giving him a chance to fess up, but he didn't take the bait. So, I said, "Anthony, I tell you what I want you to do."

"Yes sir."

"Go home, tell your mama to wash this uniform, put it in a bag, and bring it back. You will never play on this field again."

He cried, she cried, everybody cried. Remember, he was the best football player ever. As a talented peewee he scored thirty-five touchdowns in seven games. Didn't matter, though; he lied. Had he simply told the truth he would have stayed on the team.

Standing in front of hundreds of people years later, Anthony recalled that incident during his senior banquet at University of Michigan when he was asked, "Who is the toughest coach that you've ever been under? Bo Schembechler?"

"No."

"Coach Sutton."

"No."

"Well who is it?" they asked impatiently.

"The old man," Anthony said.

"Who's the old man?"

"Coach Calloway."

"What makes him so tough?"

"Not only did he put me off the baseball league," Anthony said, "but if you break one of his rules, you're going home, and may never play again. He was the best to us, but he was the toughest on us."

Anthony was voted best player to ever attend University of Michigan. My name is known in Ann Arbor because I gave them Anthony Carter. He spent thirteen amazing years in the National Football League (NFL) as one of the best who ever played the game.

My experiences on and off the field helped me relate to kids in ways few of my colleagues ever could, which made me a good coach. Coaching kids of different socio-economic backgrounds had challenges, but nothing insurmountable. I didn't judge how well a child might perform simply based on his or her talent. I had to consider their home life, relationship with parents, school performance, environment, and more.

For instance, every mother thinks her child is the best, and she should. It's important that parents make their children feel as if they can conquer the world. But know your child is no more important to another parent than theirs is to you. And your child is no more or no less in my eyes than somebody else's child. So, for me, getting to know parents was as important as getting to know the kids.

Schack Sr. and Lois Leonard had five boys, two of whom had passed away. Schack was a mechanic and an outstanding athlete in his youth. Lois was an exceptional pianist and ran a home daycare service. They attended church as a family and always appeared to be loving, involved parents. One day, Schack came by the gym to talk. He put his hand on my right shoulder and said, "Mr. Calloway, I need a promise from you."

"What you need Schack?"

"I need you to promise me you will look after my boys and take care of them."

I laughed and said, "Shaq, I always take care of the kids." I wasn't sure what he was getting at. I had worked at the gym five years and parents knew I wasn't going to do any more for their kids than I do for others. I watched over every child who walked through the gym's doors as if they were mine. Once a child came into my space, they were under my wings. I was responsible for them. But if they didn't follow the rules, they had to go.

"I need you to please promise to always look after my boys," Schack repeated with urgency. This time he had my attention.

"Schack, don't worry. I'll take care of the boys."

Three weeks later he died of a heart attack. He must have had a premonition, or he was just getting his house in order but in any event, it left me unsettled for weeks. He left the family in decent financial shape and Lois had her own income. She called me for my blessings before remarrying. The boys didn't like it and the marriage didn't last more than two years.

Over the years she called me for child-rearing advice. All the boys went to college. Schack Jr. was awarded a scholarship to a school in Virginia. Darryl was honored with a football scholarship to Florida State—a pretty big deal. He got his degree in criminal justice and worked for IBM many years. Although I helped them with fundamentals, they got into school on their own merits. Marvin is a brilliant musician who worked in the insurance industry. All three were very cerebral, reflective young men. I couldn't be any prouder of them were they my own sons. There have been so many success stories during my time in recreation that I have no doubt my steps were ordered.

My friend and colleague Bucky McGann had two children: JC and LPGA champion Michelle McGann. They have called me Uncle Dan from the time they could speak. When Michelle was young, her mother Bernadette was working fulltime and going to school for an advanced nursing degree.

Bucky brought Michelle to work from the time she could crawl. Between him, me, and our secretary Mrs. Chase, Michelle was cared for and doted over during her time at the recreation center, playing daylong with children of all races and ages. Never timid, she held her own with older kids, many of whom had rough backgrounds. You wouldn't know it now, but she was a tomboy who later became a gym rat.

We added a driving range outside the recreation complex with lights and turf. We hired a semi-pro to teach clinics. Michelle hung around him playing on the range with the balls and adult golf clubs. Daddy saw an energetic pony-tailed five-year-old swinging clubs longer than she was tall, so he went home and cut down one of his five irons.

The first time Michelle put the club in her hand and took a swing, we knew she'd play. With an intuitive rhythm only the gifted possess, she settled into her stance with unflinching confidence. Her love of the game was nurtured until she was ready to compete.

I caddied for Michelle when she won the Doherty. We were a team when as an amateur she missed the cut by one point at the LPGA US Open in Baltimore. Another time when I caddied for her at Walnut Hill Country Club in Lansing Michigan, we were leading the tournament by five shots at the twelfth. On the thirteenth hole she hit the ball at least one hundred yards from where she aimed. She asked, "Uncle Danny, where's the ball?"

I held my head low. "That ball's in the woods out of bounds."

"Uncle Danny," she said minutes later apparently flustered. "I can't feel my hands."

That was another fault of mine. I carried bananas, granola bars, and juice. I knew she must eat or drink something every four holes for her blood sugar. Diagnosed with diabetes years earlier, I should have been more aware. She was okay but she lost her lead.

I caddied for Michelle many times since she hit her first ball on the recreation center driving range. I've put thousands of talented individuals through school and coached many players who have enjoyed professional athletic careers. I put Michelle in the top five of those athletes. Another was Ottis Anderson.

Before Ottis O.J. Anderson was an NFL running back, he was a twelve-year-old toughie playing ball in the projects of West Palm Beach. His team, Young Afro Brothers of America (YABA) had no money and no financial support. They played in street clothes and old sneakers. It was reminiscent of my humble beginnings; they couldn't compete in league play without uniforms.

The fact is, the first time a child puts on a uniform, magic happens. Morale grows and a solidarity between players builds. You feel like you are a part of something bigger when everyone wears the same outfit and colors. Uniforms nurture team unity and helps to motivate players. And "when a man is sufficiently motivated," Paterson wrote, "discipline takes care of itself."

My recreation budget had an allotment for uniforms, so we kept a surplus on hand because we added teams regularly. I outfitted Ottis and his team from my surplus, and they were allowed to play in the West Palm Beach rec league. I also allowed them to participate in clinics and drills I conducted. Ottis has often said that if it weren't for those uniforms his path may have been different.

I tell the kids that come through my doors to pay it forward. If I did something good for you, I'm not looking for you to repay me. You don't owe me anything; help your brother. Everyone has stood on someone's shoulders. You didn't do it by yourself. In fact, the more successful you are, the more hands were involved to help you make it. No one is self-made. We have all crossed over a bridge that someone else built.

Retired NBA point guard Derek Harper ran basketball camps for me every year. He also gave his name for the Christmas basketball tournaments at the schools. Derek was the second of nine kids. He rode his bike from West Palm to the Riviera gym.

One day I saw him peek with curiosity through the gym door. "What's your name son?"

"Whopper," he said shyly. "Came here to see the camp." ABA professional Levern Tart was conducting a basketball camp.

"Come on in my boy."

When he was in high school, I'd take him and a small group of guys to dinner. They'd look openmouthed at the food and ask for two pieces of meat. Their homes didn't supply an endless supply of groceries. Whenever I saw Derek, I'd pass him a fifty for food. Third year of college Derek called me to ask my advice about coming out under the hardship draft, which allows a player to request permission to join an NBA team without completing college. The player must prove he is a hardship case based on a financial or other condition. I told him he needs his stepfather to handle that. He told me, "No. I need you to make the decision because you've always done that for me." He was in the draft with Michael Jordan and offered a million-dollar contract. I told him to come on out.

Ottis was a star at Forest Hill High School breaking records left and right. During summer break from the University of Miami, he joined Lamar to conduct sports clinics at my camps. His generous financial support has breathed life into many of the Youth Recreation Association's initiatives. Ottis rushed for 193 yards in his debut NFL game, one of the best starts in the League's history. And for all his accolades, his older brother was as good a player.

Marvin, or Smokey as he was called, might have been a better ball player than Ottis. His parents came from Riviera and wanted me to decide where Marvin should play college ball. I told Marvin he should go to Florida A&M but assured him no freshman played on the team, no matter how good they were. The coach had an outstanding bench and didn't lack for talented players. In other words, Marvin would have to sit out his freshman year. They offered him a job in the laundromat to help with expenses. Like most elite athletes who want no part of the bench, he balked at not being able to play.

Arkansas offered him the same package but would allow him to play as a freshman. Every athlete wants to play. No one wants to wait their time. I gave in to him, though it was more of a cause to his family. Subsequently, he had a standout season, receiving freshman of the year in the southwest conference.

In the spring he and friends went swimming. The water looked like silk, smooth and lustrous. Marvin dove in the water, unaware the depths. He hit his head just beneath the surface and broke his neck. He never came out of the coma. It took me fifteen years to get over his death. I wanted him to go to A&M. I allowed Marvin to persuade me from what I knew to be best for him. For fifteen years I blamed myself for his death.

Another time, I had sent four outstanding athletes off to Kentucky State. James Potbelly Jackson, on the roster to play a tournament that summer in Connecticut, was one of the athletes. He was playing a pick-up game with friends, slid off someone's back and suffered a concussion. He was in the hospital for six weeks with bleeding on the brain. His mother had two young kids, no insurance, no income. The city paid most of the bill; I covered the balance.

When it was time to leave for Connecticut, I left him home because I thought he wasn't healthy enough to travel or play. The doctor said he could not participate in organized ball. Besides, he hadn't fully recovered from his injury. A nag within me said I should have sent him to college with the others, but I knew the doctors said he could not play. At that point in my life, I knew not to second guess myself. Make the decision and stand by it. Second semester he would be better.

So, the three young men left for school and were doing well. James missed his friends, got down on himself because he was injured, and got mixed up with a bad crowd. He and three boys robbed the army navy store. The police descended on the area, lights flashing, weapons drawn. Two of the boys got away, one got shot. James, hiding in the store, was thought to have a gun in his hand. He was shot three times and instantly killed.

That was a sad day for me. I told myself, if only I had sent him to the school, red-shirted him—just let him be there—this might not have happened. "IF," such a small word that holds one in its clutches with immense power. "IF" is the devil's epee, slashing the spirit with stiff reproach. I spent sleepless nights tossing around in my mind many scenarios, thinking had I done this or that Marvin and James might still be alive. It took a long time to reconcile my role in their deaths, that the plans of the Lord stand firm, whether I understand or not.

Most my life everyone came to me to make decisions for them. That was my lot. I didn't begrudge it, nor did I take it for granted. Every so often things happen that ask you to question the whys of life. But you must stand by your decisions. What's done is done. You cannot turn back time. Sometimes it's best to make an unwise decision than no decision at all. There was never middle with me. Black and white. Yes or no. Do or don't.

As assistant recreation director I was in charge of all the programs, tournaments, AAU basketball. My kids competed in Connecticut one year. The following year I took thirty children to Indiana: fifteen whites and fifteen blacks. I put a black and white in each room, so they'd get to know each other. Part of our itinerary was guests of the Chicago Cubs at Wrigley Fields. Our names sparkled brightly on the Marquee as we entered the stadium: Welcome Dan Calloway and the Tate Eagles from Riviera Florida. You could see us on the Jumbotron. It was an exceptional experience based on a decision I made to travel as a team instead of staying local.

I had three ball boys. Dane, Douglas, and one other. I played ball with their father in West Palm Beach. They were two white boys who traveled with a busload of older Black boys. The parents entrusted me with their boys traversing the country. I put black and white together because it was important for me to have them know they were the same.

American Legion Post 12 had no Blacks on their teams long after integration. Legion ball is the highest you can go before heading to college or signing in the pros. But Blacks in segregation couldn't play Legion ball. I told their coach my kids were better than anyone on their team. I suggested my players Alfred, James, and Larry, to integrate Legion Ball. At the time Blacks played ball in the Orange State championships. Every year they held championships up in Orlando. Well, he took my guys and they won the southern region district. That is why I do what I do.

There were plenty logistical challenges when I took youth out of state for more than a day: how to transport them, where will they sleep, how many chaperones are needed, how much do I budget, insurance, food. There are many moving parts. While in the army I organized large tournaments and events. Although I had a staff to handle the details, I still had to produce the plans. It was similar to how Bucky and I operated. But the city didn't care and in August 1973, Bucky McGann was unjustly relieved of his duties.

City council members thought they were doing me a favor by firing Bucky and offering me the directorship. They didn't care that he and I had a proven system, that we ran a tight ship, and the children loved us. Bucky handled administrative tasks; I controlled operations. He had a business background from Notre Dame; I knew how to make everybody look good.

So, with Bucky out, I left too. We went into business together, running lawn maintenance and janitorial companies for two years.

The Great Muhammad Ali

BEFORE THE CALLOWAY COMPLEX, Tate gym was used for many community functions, and benefitted from nationally televised news and events. It was an exciting place where something was always happening. When President James Earl Carter Jr. campaigned for reelection, the late police chief Boone Darden brought in Muhammed Ali who stumped for Carter.

Boone was an exceptional community relations-officer and eloquent spokesman. In his white three-piece suits, he hugged babies and mothers with the tenderness of a doting father. No one was afraid to talk to him because he was so engaged. He visited storefronts and nursing homes, schools, and churches. He personified how a good officer conducts himself in the community: non-confrontational and sincere. He acted like he cared about the people.

At the time I was in the Sheriff's office and the city called on me to help put together a nice program. I organized an exhibition match and found two or three men eager to spar against him. Ali shuffled into the gym front toe heel back punching the air toward men lining the walls. He pulled a man into a headlock and aired his head like he was in a WWE match.

The audience erupted in applause and chants of "Ali. Ali. Ali!" All the while, Ali is asking, "Where's Dan? I'm looking for the poor fool called Dan." Someone told him I put the exhibition together and mistakenly thought he was going to spar me. When he realized I wasn't going in the ring with him, he challenged me to a three-point shoot.

"Old man, I can beat you," Muhammed said, talking smack.

"Hold it just a minute," I said.

"You know where I'm from?" Ali asked.

"Yeah, you're from Louisville."

"You know what happens in Louisville?"

"Yeah. Greasy chicken and cheap bourbon." I knew what he was driving at, but I can kid with the best of them, including Muhammad Ali. He smiled a "gonna knock you out" smile and took an air punch. Even those stung.

He warmed up in front of thousands of googly-eyed spectators: three buckets, four bricks. Lucky number seven. I begged him to move closer to the free-throw line. I knew he was going down. He might be king of the ring, but this was my house. Honestly, I know me. I didn't plan to take it easy on him and didn't want to embarrass him.

"Why don't you move closer to the fans?" I asked.

"Oh no... if you can shoot from back here, so can I," he said.

We played first to ten. Of course, I knocked down ten out of eleven. Muhammad barely hit the rim. "I can't believe an old man like you can shoot like that," he said.

"Who you think built this gym?" I asked. "Don't you know I walk in here and say, 'Gym, Dan Calloway's here. Let me knock some down.'"

I'm teasing with him. He's joking around like a big kid. People are laughing but they didn't come to see me. They came to see the great Muhammad Ali, who I just beat ten to three in a three-point shoot-out. Five thousand people in the middle of the day. He entered the ring softly punching one of the men, picture taken, round one, done. The next one comes in, punch the chest softly, cameras clicking, round two, done. They were playing to the press.

Then James, half a Muslim with boxing dreams, gets into the ring, and really starts hitting Ali. Who would risk getting hit over the head by the greatest boxer who ever lived? Muhammad wasn't impressed. In fact, I saw his fist balling.

"Dan, what's the matter with this fool?" Ali asked me.

I hollered, "James, not now. Leave him alone." He had begged me to let him go one round. He had recently changed his name and wanted to impress Ali that he could really box. Herman said, "I told you he was gonna act out."

Well Ali put his left hand over James's head, wound up his right hand like he was about to kill the fool. He was just playing but I pulled James out anyway. Round three. TKO.

Everybody had a camera, national and local media clamoring for attention, fans trying to get autographs, babies screaming, kids sparring in fun. It was the biggest thing that ever happened in little Riviera. Boone, Ali, and I kept the crowd happy. We allowed as many photo opportunities as possible with "The Greatest." President Carter wasn't mentioned once.

Youth Recreation Association

YRA HAS BEEN A 501c3 for over fifty years. We have sent more individuals to college, fed more people, and uniformed more adolescents than any organization in Florida.

I drew up plans for the Youth Recreation Association because I realized much more needed to be done than I was able to do through the city. Lamar Parrish was graduating from high school and had a scholarship to go to Lincoln University of Missouri, a HBCU founded by black veterans of the Civil War. I knew his family didn't have enough money to put him on the bus to Jupiter much less St. Louis Missouri.

I called around and raised money to make sure we could buy winter clothes and books. There were five or ten of us that put money in the pot to afford necessities. The money we made we kept in the coffers. We raised funds during tag day, sold chicken dinners and dessert. We'd wear our uniforms and solicit money on the street. We raised enough to send Lamar to college and to put warm clothes on his back.

Lamar's athletic career started as a nine-year-old who followed me around the dirt roads of Riviera Beach as a child, conducted camps for me every year. I considered him a little brother, choosing him as my teammate when we played sandlot baseball. At ten, he wasn't afraid to play the men. He was a big boy for his age. We could tell he had natural talent, not only his quickness, but his hands.

Most kids at ten, unless they are exceptional, don't have coordination; they grow into it in their teens. Touch football with men ten and twelve years his senior and he was never afraid. He was one of those rare kids who listened. Whenever we explained a play to him, he'd execute it perfectly. Few people had more talent. He was known for his football, track and field talent throughout high school, college, and the NFL. He was a tremendous basketball and baseball player. But most of all, out of all the kids I've handled, he is most like me in that he had the ability to teach and coach kids without making them feel they had to live up to his reputation.

The hardest thing for a person with a great deal of athletic ability to do is to look at a child objectively, without judging their talent against his. I learned early in my coaching career that not everyone was able to do something just because I could.

Sam Smith, one of my caddies when I was caddie master, drove home that lesson. At times, the men exhibited behaviors and attitudes that I considered unacceptable. Mediocrity has no place in my presence. I wanted them to be the best at all times, not just when someone handed them a dollar. One day Sam asked me for a meeting. He called me "Mr. Calloway" even though he was closer to Daddy's age.

"Its's out of respect for your position," he said. "You know Mr. Calloway; us caddies always do our best for you so you will look good. We know what you expect from us."

He told me he watched me coach his sons in baseball. His son Darryl was an outstanding athlete. "You were always hard on my kids and their teammates. Everybody don't have the talent and the ability to do what you do."

I listened and meditated on what he said. Then recycled his words in my mind. As it sunk in, it hit me hard. I was driven to be the best and expected everyone else to follow suit. Coach Brooks use to infuriate me because he allowed anyone on the team. He pulled me aside and said, "Calloway, you must understand. We're teaching kids. The reason to carry all these kids is they might actually learn how to be dedicated and give their all. Participation is the way they will learn. I know most of these kids ain't going to the leagues, but son, it gives them hope. It gives them something to look back on."

I can help you hone your talent. But you must put in the work.

Early in my career, I refused to coach girls. I knew I'd be as strict on them as I was on the boys, and honestly, I didn't think they could condition their bodies as well. If you are dedicated enough to train your body, then I can teach you how to become a complete athlete. But there are no shortcuts. Every ounce of mettle must be earned.

Well, my girls earned my trust and proved to me that they can perform under pressure as well as if not better than their male counterparts. My team was playing in the Magic Johnson Adidas Classic in Lansing Michigan. There to compete were seventy-six top female teams from around the country. Even though we had won two years earlier in Columbus Ohio, we were still little known. We played Jackie Joyner Kersey's team, Primetime, winner of ninety-one games in a row.

Everyone was talking about Primetime and their winning record. Never on a stage this big before, my team handled the pressure and outplayed the other team. Every inning my girls matched Kersey's team play for play and left Michigan as champs. My team performed at their peak by becoming masters of the non-negotiables:

1.Learn the fundamentals

2.Respect the rules

3.Be in impeccable condition

You can have all the talent in the world, but if you don't master the basics, you never move from good to better. I can teach you the fundamentals, but you have to put in the work and practice. Even elite athletes train on the rudiments of the game.

Rule number one: you must be on time. If my bus is scheduled to leave at six o'clock, we're easing down the road at six o one. I've lost games for leaving players behind. Delta won't let you on the plane once the jet bridge door is shut. You must be on time.

When I was a sophomore in high school, we were headed to Tampa for a championship football game. One of the trainers asked, "Everybody on the bus?" I answered, "Everybody but George." George, a senior, was the star quarterback headed to an elite college on scholarship. Coach cranked up the bus, pulled off, taking two lefts. A mile down the road someone yelled, "Coach, George is running down the hill with his equipment." The coach didn't say a word, just kept driving. George never played on the team again. He lost his scholarship too.

I can teach you everything you need to succeed except courage and perseverance. Those are muscles you must develop.

But there are no shortcuts. He who shuns the dust of the arena, shall not sit in the shade of the olive tree. You can't enjoy the breeze and a glass of iced tea with me until you enter the arena and fight as if your life is on the line. I have fought the battle. Now you must put in the work. No short cut allowed.

It doesn't matter what sport you play, if you aren't conditioned, you lose your wind, your legs give out, you give in. Stamina is increased by running. I always wanted my teams to outlast the competition. You don't have to have all the talent to be in good condition. I run my teams so they can fight until the final second. Eight decades later, I'm still in the ring. Stamina.

I stopped basing the merit of success on talent and started looking at how well my athletes handled pressure. When I think back on the athletes who set themselves apart, few attributes distinguished them from the average players more than their ability to handle pressure. A lot of people have talent, but when they compete against people who have the same amount of talent or more, who prevails? The one who hangs in there and refuses to give up. You must tell yourself you will fight through the final second, even when all hope looks lost. It takes courage to fight to the finish. Fear ruins more careers than do injuries.

My players and I were playing a game in a gym where we were the only black team. Our sponsor was White, and he was suffering the same abuse. The Lake Worth gym was filled with gun-toting men and it got nasty in there. My team got a little rattled and intimidated by the guns, so I called time out.

"What Y'all so afraid of? Get your head out your tails and get on that floor and fight!"

We won the game by more than sixty points and never played them again.

The Bill Russell basketball tournament was rolling around. The assistant director was from the Glades. He remembered me and invited us to join the tournament. We coordinated the trip but first had to raise money. We had a few big benefactors and I was honored with the Dan Calloway Day which was a great honor for me. The marquis on the Big Dollar Grocery Store read: "Closed. Today we are honoring Dan Calloway Day, Riviera Son." Thirteen hundred people in the high school gym. The capacity was seven hundred. We charged a dollar entry fee, sold food and drinks, and made enough to rent a Greyhound bus for me to take the softball team to the tournament in Connecticut. The kids were entrusted to me for a week and I had to prove myself to the families.

This was our first trip out of state, and it taught me how to administrate and coordinate later trips. Eighty kids came for try-outs. We kept thirty. Every day for six weeks I ran drills and practice. Then, the big day. If you heard me shouting

"Bingo!" that meant we dropped baskets left and right. Picture us in tight shorts and floppy afros. We put on a display. Fans turned on the referees because they were making bad calls against us. But we won handily in double overtime and the invitations began pouring in for us to participate in future AAU tournaments around the country. Since then, we've been instrumental in sending many children to college and to the pros.

I inherited the Tate Eagles who became the Calloway Angels. We played Black America Softball Association (BASA) and AAU tournaments. When we went to the Bahamas the Prime Minister invited me to speak to their Law Enforcement officers about our Police Athletic League. The Angels may be the most successful program I've ever had. But the Angels sustained their top rank for eight years because they put in the work.

The league in Minnesota paid part of our plane fare so we'd make it there for the championships. They used our name as a draw to attract the best teams in the nation. We practiced from the first week in February each year. To help with expenses, they had to sell raffles, and hold baskets like boots on street corners. We sold dinners also. We always managed to make it from one game to the next. My girls had to follow rules like everyone else:

1. Don't drink
2. Don't smoke
3. Be on time
4. Don't get pregnant

I've coached hundreds of young women and had only one get pregnant. I was a disciplinarian. If I told you to run until I was tired, but you only ran until you got tired, then you didn't make the cut. When I say jump, you better not hop. If you weren't where I said to be at the time I said, you got left. Out of town on weekends, we're going to someone's Sunday service. Whenever we went out, they had to dress and look like ladies. Those were my rules. If they didn't follow the rules, they were off the team.

Grace was an all-American, rated in the top ten female softball players in the nation. She traveled with BASA all over the country. When she graduated from college, she told everyone her daddy, Dan Calloway, was instrumental in her success. The captain, Melva, is an attorney. Gail works at Cape Canaveral and her daughters have college degrees. Shawn is a CPA. Althea, Lucy, Grace are police officers. Tabitha teaches elementary school. The girls were with me between ten and thirty years. I've attended graduations, weddings, births, funerals, retirements. I walked two of the girls down the aisle. I was a proud poppa.

Our Optimist and Little League included kids eight to twelve years old. I was teaching them how to be good athletes as well as a good citizen. The rules of life and the rules of the game are similar. When there are rules you must follow them. Every game has rules and regulations. Balls and strikes, outs, and penalties.

The same thing in life. If you respect the rules, you're okay. If you violate them, you get the whistle. Little kids are sponges.

The ones who develop quickly are those who listen without losing their train of thought. So, as coach, instructor, parent, you must understand a child's spirit is easily crushed if you teach them the wrong fundamentals. There are two things children must master before they can move forward.

1. Do unto other as you would have them do unto you
2. Obey the rules

The only people that get in trouble are the ones who break the rules. It's that simple. Stop overcomplicating things. Adjust to the law and don't break the rules. The person who says, "Bump the rules," is the one who down the line gets caught, goes to jail, or gets killed. When you have no regard for the law, you have two ways to go: jail or the graveyard.

If you talk when I'm trying to talk, and not pay attention, you think I'm going to let you put on this uniform and bring harm to the team or yourself because I know you're not listening. If we call a play to the left and you run to the right you're going to get killed over there. You don't have any support, no blockers, no one running interference for you.

I have served as surrogate father to kids and adults for many years. I always had Mama and Daddy. Eighty percent of the kids I have nurtured over the years have only had me and their teammates as family. Unfortunately, sometimes the parents lack basic fundamentals. What do you do? You show up for them too.

I was in the kid's lives from day one. They came to me about everything from school, girls, jobs, and more. Bruce got his undergraduate degree and got in a little trouble. His family had no insurance, he lost his job. His problem got worse and he needed intervention. I spent thousands of dollars out of pocket to get him help and it was the best money I ever spent. Years later he went back to school for his master's degree, and when they called for his family, it was my name they called. It was a proud moment for me.

I could recall hundreds of stories like the ones I've shared. The circumstances might differ, but the root is all the same. Those children either didn't have supportive mothers or fathers, their parents put them in my hands, or I recognized talent and took them under wing on my own. Sometimes a child has it all and still needs a little more support and guidance. That is why you must get to know your families, not only the children.

I've had legions of generous benefactors who have helped me do what I do. All-American Tucker Fredrickson, former running back for the New York Giants and first overall pick in the 1965 NFL draft has supported the Association in myriad ways. I could never thank him enough. From business mogul Don Donagher to athletes like NFL linebacker Ricky Jackson, and friends like Doc Helms, each used time, name, and energy to help uplift the lives of thousands of YRA student athletes for over fifty years.

Palm Beach Sports Hall of Fame

MY PROFESSIONAL BASEBALL CAREER was cut short due to injury, not the inability to live out the dreams everyone had for me. God had other plans for my life.

I've lived long enough to know athletic ability erodes quickly. Thirty-five, forty years of age it's gone. But when you study human nature and the tendencies, norms, and mores of society, you can change the world. In other words, can you still light up the world once the spotlight turns off?

I've been asked, "How do you get along with all those wealthy people?" My answer is simple: "I don't look at them as wealthy people, I see them as friends." Wealth is subjective. You can be poor when you live solely for yourself, and you can be wealthy when you touch peoples' lives. You can't take your money with you, but I guarantee your legacy lives on. When I go to the grave, somebody is going to remember something good I did along the way. If you're lucky like me, you get to smell your flowers while living.

Herman McCray paid me the greatest compliment I've ever received. A group was discussing what they'd do if they won the lottery, each naming off extravagances like homes, cars, and travel. "Man, what you gonna do?" they asked Herman.

"I'm gonna give it to Dan Calloway."

"Why would you give it to that crazy man?" they asked.

Herman said, "Because he'd spend it on people who need it."

"That's exactly why I wouldn't give it to him," said one of the men. "I know the fool would give it away."

A similar compliment was paid to me when in 1992 I joined the ranks of sports icons Jack Nicklaus, Lamar Parrish, Hank Aaron, and other men and women who had played professional sports in the county.

Before the official recognition Sportscaster Jim Gallagher said this of me to the audience: "If this man decides to run for elected office, I guarantee he'll win by a landslide. He may be the most popular person you've never heard of in Palm Beach County." His words were truer than he knew. However, despite advocating for the poor, feeding the hungry, and sitting with Presidents, I have never had a desire for politics.

Filipe Alou, Barry Hill, Stranahan, and I were soon inducted into the elite membership of the Palm Beach County Sports Hall of Fame. I was recognized for a lifetime of contributions in sports. Don Wilson introduced me. He taught school for forty years, served as councilman, and was one of the finest people I knew, always making others feel good, no matter the situation. When he formally welcomed me as a 1992 inductee in the Palm Beach Sports Hall of Fame, he said, "Dan Calloway has the ability to walk and talk with presidents and potentates, wine and dine with kings and queens, but he will never lose the common touch."

He couldn't have depicted me better. I am in awe of no one, but respectful of everyone. If you put me in an alley with a man drinking wild turkey hustling stale donuts, I'll be the same with him as if sitting with the POTUS. I am the same yesterday, today, and tomorrow. If I look down, I am trying to pick you up. If I look up, I am trying to put you back in your rightful place. Right, wrong, good, or bad, that is how I lived my life.

CALLOWAY STRONG

Bernard

Buck was constantly teaching me. He had less athletic ability, but he was the smartest and kindest. I was always the youngest on the same teams with brothers and the better player. If Buck was up to bat and struck out, I'd ask him, "How could you go up there and strike out?" Or if another player missed a catch I'd ask, "How could you drop the ball? Don't you know how to catch?"

I'm three, four years younger than my teammates and yelling at them because I don't want to lose. I'm upset because they're not playing well. We'd get home and Buck would tell me, "Danny, you got to stop being so hotheaded. That's human nature. People gonna always make mistakes." His constancy was an ever-present help.

We had chores every day. Cut the lawn, sweep off the porch, rake the yard, trim the wicks, wipe down the kitchen. Mama didn't have to clean the house or cook. The oldest boy would have dinner waiting. We'd do our chores early because we took a daily nap until the age of fifteen. As soon as two o'clock rolled around—the heat of the day—I'd shake Buck awake.

"Come on Buck. Come outside and warm me up."

"Aww man. I don't feel like doing it right now."

"Buck, you got to warm me up." Now I'm getting annoyed because he knows how important it is for me to practice. When he got older and went to work, I'd pull Faye out there. She didn't know what she was doing but I taught her enough so she could at least throw the ball where I could hit grounders. I was driven to always practice my craft. And Buck was usually the one on the other end of the ball.

Yes, its true I took a nap every day. I didn't have to, but my health teacher said, "If you eat carrots, you'll have pretty eyes. If you eat beets, you'll have strong blood. If you smoke or drink alcohol, you will never be a good athlete. It will kill your coordination. An apple a day will keep the doctor away."

I begged Mama to get apples for Buck to pack in my lunch. Mama told us, "If you sleep one or two hours in the afternoon, you'll grow to be big and strong." Remember, I'm youngest of my three brothers, so I made sure to sleep so I'd be as strong or stronger than my brothers. Turns out all our "mothers" told us the same gobbledygook and I bought into it hook, line, sinker.

Daddy bought an old car for Buck when he graduated high school. If we were poor, we couldn't convince anyone we knew. How many poor folks get cars as graduation presents? When it was time for me to graduate, I knew my car was coming but I told Mama to get me a good suitcase instead. When I graduated, I was presented with gray hard side American Tourister luggage. I was heading for major leagues; I wanted to be ready. Nonetheless, in 1957, the year after I graduated, Buck and I bought a car together: a brand spanking new black Chevrolet.

"Come on, let's go for a ride," Buck said.

"Okay man, let me polish my shoes."

Buck, Faye, and I were in the living room listening to the radio. Mama and Daddy told us to never polish our shoes in the living room, but I didn't want to miss the "Hit Parade." Faye and Buck said, "Don't come in here with that."

"I got the paper, it's gonna be alright."

Well, I took everything out the shoeshine box, layered the newspaper on the floor, and kicked over the open bottle of polish. It ran off the paper and onto the rug. "You gonna get a whipping," Faye said. We got as much of it up as we could, then I moved the corner of the couch over the area that stained. I was too big for Daddy to whoop, but when he found out he grated on my nerves so badly I'd have taken the whooping!

April 2, 1960 Buck joined the Army. During his first furlough home, on June 16 he married an old classmate of mine, Freddie. He was in the service when the Berlin Crisis broke out and his term was extended by six months. We stayed in touch by letter, until I was drafted and joined him in the ranks.

He was in a tank unit when I received a letter of concern: he had frostbite and almost lost his toes. I went to the General and asked if he could help get Buck out the field. He pulled rank and Buck was reassigned until his discharge.

I can't say why things happen the way they do but therein lies the mystery of life, figuring out what to figure out. When Buck got sick, it was not for me to question why.

Buck wore shorts to work every day. I was visiting with him at his fish market when I noticed a roach-like growth on the back of his leg. By the time he got the carcinoma checked it had already spread. Fortunately, his cancer went into remission for two years.

My brother was my friend. His death affected me harder than any other. As long as I can remember, I had Buck. He was my anchor. He taught me to recite every bible verse at school. We studied spelling bee words together as we ate butter-fried Spam sandwiches in the noisy lunchroom.

When I dedicated my life to sports, he and Faye became my biggest cheerleaders, encouraging me to never give up on my dreams. If you are fortunate enough to have people in your life who champions you the way my family supported me, count yourself blessed among nations.

Advocate for someone who needs you. Mama taught me about the bird and bees and that my word was my bond. Daddy taught me though life's sand traps are unavoidable, you can still save par. He taught me that a job well done is a job worth doing. But it was Buck who taught me the fundamentals of a well-lived life. He was my best friend. I took Buck's death harder than any. But I feel him telling me, "thank you little brother; all is well."

Junior

When Junior had his stroke, we took his car keys and bought him a bike. It was a tough decision, but he went along with it. Every morning he rode his red bicycle to Faye's, cut her lawn, trimmed her hedges, made sure her porch light worked. He did the same at my house, then helped Buck half a day at the fish market.

Evenings he'd have dinner prepared for everyone. The stroke he suffered years earlier left him with a speech impairment, so he communicated with few words. "Eat." "Go." "What to do?"

I knew what he said when others didn't, and he never regained full control of his speech center.

Every year Junior, Mama and I went to the Ebony Fashion Fair, a pageant of extravagant couture and pomp, popular with Black middle-class women and men. For fifty-years, Ebony Magazine took the show on the road and featured European and Afro-centric high fashions. When the show came here it was special for me and Junior to take Mama as our date.

Junior took loving care of Mama, cooking and cleaning and caring for her with a level of uncommon devotion. Before Mama died, Junior began to look tired but continued to cook and clean. Mama, by now in declining health, became his reason for living. And still, he smiled a toothless smile and pedaled on down the road.

A couple weeks after mama died, Faye called.

"Danny, I need you to check on Gene. He's lost a lot of weight." I thought he had a tough time because of mama's death.

He set the gold standard for how we, as siblings, care for one another. He took pride in his role as big brother. It was one of his greatest achievements. When we were younger, our age difference kept us from doing more together. As a child, I grated Gene's nerves. Outside of the time he beat me with Mama's brush, he was actually pretty forgiving of my troublesome ways.

Looking back, I know Daddy and Mama indulged me more than the others. I was the baby boy and enjoyed the spoils of the position. I did more than any other with Daddy, though he taught all of us to play golf. He'd take Gene to the course and lay into him if he didn't play well. Then, they'd come home, and Daddy would keep on. "How could you lose the damn ball?"

I asked him, "Daddy, how can you do that to Junior? You know he doesn't care nothing about playing. He's just going out there to spend time with you."

I told Junior, "Get away from him. You don't need that." Junior was the bigger man, although he was stubborn too. There was no fist-fighting, but they had a battle of wills. Daddy wanted things done his way or the highway. He was a fusser, harping on and on about the littlest thing. Well, Daddy won. Junior left at eighteen because he had had enough.

Everything I did as an adult, Gene was there, cheering me on like a devoted big brother. His graduation present to me was a trip to the 1956 World Series played between the New York Yankees and defending champion Brooklyn Dodgers, my favorite team. Forever the big brother, he supported my dreams and was excited he could do something so extravagant.

He was living in Nantucket and looking forward to taking me to see icons of the game. Even though West Palm Beach was a spring training hub and I had seen many of the game's legends while watching exhibition games from behind the fence, nothing compared to being in the big arena.

Gene took me to my first professional game at Ebbets Field in Brooklyn and Yankee Stadium in the Bronx. These were rivalry games played between the two New York City teams, the Yankees and Mets and part of the subway series. Just looking at a major league ballpark was an unbelievable experience.

What you see on television versus what you see in person lies a world apart. In person you are surrounded by forty, fifty thousand adoring fans screaming and cheering their teams on. The reverberation is deafening but unbelievably inspiring for a young person who has dreams a becoming a professional athlete.

Junior was a really good athlete. He had great hand-eye coordination and could have exceled at any sport had he stayed in school. He worked at Howard Johnson with Mama and became a really good cook. He traveled north to cook at resorts in the summers.

All my life I needed to be able to step in the gap to take care of my sister, my brothers, and my parents. Didn't matter that I was the youngest boy. God ordained me keeper of the ark. When Daddy died, I had Gene live with Mama. He took loving care of her and became an irreplaceable big brother. He felt bad he wasn't around in my heyday, but he made up for it in his later years.

Faye was right, he didn't look well. I took him to the VA and his doctors ran a barrage of tests. Six hours later, they came in and told us he had colon cancer that metastasized to other parts of his body. He was given two months to live. He lived four.

Gene and I had strengthened our relationship over the years. In fact, long before he died, we shared conversations and laughs that might make you blush. But we'll keep those between us.

Willie Ellis

WHEN HONEYMAN COLLAPSED IN the bathroom doorway, I was raking palm leaves and twigs out the front yard. Faye yelled for me to come in. "Danny, Honeyman needs you." I rushed in and saw my brother gripping the doorframe. Honeyman clung to the edge of two worlds, his breath rested on the ether.

He had been complaining of headaches for years, but he was such a brute we brushed it off and thought he was trying to get out of doing chores. The doctors at Pine Ridge treated him for bad sinuses. Every day Honeyman swallowed a handful of horse pills, which was supposed to treat his condition.

I was fifteen, he twenty. Our wills battled since birth. We butted heads like big horn sheep. We rivaled on and off the court, probably because Daddy pitted me so often against my brothers without cause.

"Why can't you be like your little brother?" he'd ask.

Gene could take it, Buck gladly ignored it, but it crawled under Honeyman's skin like a bad itch. It made for really poor bedfellows.

"You had the same opportunity but you're lazy."

Daddy didn't know anything was wrong with Honeyman. No one did. However, the fact is, I don't think Willie Ellis believed enough in his abilities though he was an outstanding athlete. I actually felt sorry for him. He not only heard it at home, but he got it in the streets too. Girls approached him often only to say something about me.

"I saw your brother playing with the men last Sunday. He's some kind of ball player." That really stabbed at him. He was so jealous he started fights with me all the time. Comparison is the thief of joy and the whip that snaps at the mule.

"You think you're so much. You're not better than me."

"Then why you not playing with the Tigers?"

I had no problem goading him. In fact, for a long time, I took pleasure in it. I loved that he lived in my sun. Five years younger and I played ball with him in the junior leagues and made all star in school sports. Whatever he did, I made sure I did better.

Despite it all, when I held Honeyman in my arms that day we were Calloway Strong. I couldn't have loved him more. Two and a half hours; that's a long time to watch someone die. The previous night he hung out at the juke. An hour before he knocked on heaven's door, he sat at the table eating Cornflakes.

Mama and Daddy in transit; Buck bagging groceries in West Palm Beach, Gene in Korea fighting a forgotten war. Two funeral homes competed for the dead while a scared teenaged girl called from the list of emergency numbers taped near the rotary phone.

The segregated south in the woods. An untimely place for emergencies. A loathsome place to be sick. When Mama walked through the door, me holding Honeyman's limp body, faint breath ascending the rafters, she screamed, "What happened to my boy?" Daddy and I put him in the back seat, and they rushed to the hospital. Two white stops later, there was nothing more to be done when they arrived at Pine Ridge. The spirit returned to God who gave it.

"He's gone," Mama said, as she walked through the door. Then she fell on the bed, no good for months. Faye cried for weeks. Buck could make no sense of it. Gene remained overseas. Daddy put on a good face, but it was hard.

"They want to do an autopsy," Mama said.

"Mama, you have to let them do it. How else will we know?"

"No son of mine is getting his head cut open," Daddy said.

"But Daddy, that's the only way we'll know what happened."

They speculated a pea-sized mass turned into a baseball-sized tumor. Maybe growing there for five years. When he said he was having headaches, he wasn't lying. I should have believed him. Mama grieved for three months. She barely worked her job. It took Buck some time to get over it, too. I didn't shed a tear, yet I longed to tackle him once again in the white sand where we lay his body to rest.

"Danny," Mama said.

"Yes Mama."

"You're in charge now."

Sleep Eternal Peace

I WAS THE BULLDOG, the person everyone called if they needed something done. This was especially true in my family. Daddy had been increasingly sick, and Mama had trouble getting him to eat or take his pills. "If you don't take your medicine, I have to call Danny." He grumbled until Mama called me.

"Daddy," I said. "I need you to take your medicine and eat your food, so I won't have to take you to the hospital."

I held the hospital over his head because he hated to go. Chances are Daddy grew up hearing "the system" doesn't help black people. Many in his generation fell headfirst into the belief that "something's wrong" with medical establishments. Similar to people who kept money in mattresses and out of banks, our history of distrust isn't baseless.

America has an ugly past of unspeakable experimentation and morally bankrupt treatments on patients unawares. There was also the deceptive narrative that Blacks were innately inferior to Whites, both physically and mentally. For many years, Whites couldn't even receive a Black person's blood for transfusion for fear of becoming "tainted." Is it a wonder Daddy was hesitant? Not to worry. God has his way.

When the town was really small, there was a Methodist, Baptist, and Sanctified church. You went to one or the other and your business was your neighbors' gossip. As the town grew, nobody knew him; his peers had either died or moved north during the Great Migration.

Even though his Volkswagen Beetle license plate spelled "ROB," no one remembered his name. He'd come home complaining about how badly he had been treated by people whose parents' noses he had wiped many years ago. He didn't change with the times and the times caught up to him.

Still, he refused to comply. He had lived his life on his terms, no worse for the wear, able to care for his wife and children as he thought he would when purveying the land that rained bread from heaven.

He wasn't bedridden though, still able to drive to Dunkin Donuts for his coffee and donut under dawn's buttery gleam. I think he needed one last hoorah, a ride through the town that had given him so much. His special place where ancestral dreams washed ashore unfettered, speaking in native tongue, "Akwaaba." Welcome.

The following Friday, December 5, 1987 he died of natural causes in his sleep.

I had lived with Mama and Daddy until I moved into my own home on 34th Street at the age of thirty-four. Mama had been telling me for a few years, "The old lady is not going to be here long. Take care of your brothers and sister." She was preparing me for the inevitable, but I couldn't see the snake for the bush, even though I had been taking mama for blood transfusions every week.

On one of my last trips to the clinic with her I said, "Mama if you don't tell me what's going on, I'm going in the doctor's room with you."

She said, "You'll do no such thing. That's business and my business only."

"Yes I am. You go in there when I'm sick," I said.

"That's different; I'm the mama."

Even in my sixties I would never argue with my mother, I can tell you that. I respected her word. She eventually told us she had been sick with leukemia for the past two years or so. We never noticed because she never let on, same tender smile, same charitable spirit.

Mama believed with all her heart the words spoken in Matthew 11. "Come unto me, all you who labor and are heavy laden, and I will give you rest." Not once did she waver in faith, though the load she carried was heavy. She suffered gladly. The joy of the Lord was her strength.

Does a child ever fully understand the sacrifices of a mother, of a parent? To reflect on my life without acknowledging the stand Mama took for the sake of her children would be the worse injustice imaginable. The dress she shielded us under as the Ku Klux Klan neared is committed to memory. At eight years old I told her, "Just wait until I grow up Mama; I'll protect you." God gave me a lifetime to do just that.

Mama's illness went downhill quickly. We turned her bedroom into a hospital room. Home Hospice showed us how to nurse her. Gene had lived with Mama since his stroke years earlier. He prepared breakfast and lunch and kept the house clean. I helped in the evenings.

She told me I was in charge of her will. She didn't need a will because her children would do exactly what she tells me to do, but she wanted no misunderstandings. The bit of money she had wasn't worth talking about. The house in which she and Gene lived was left for Faye and she could rent, sell, or live in it to help get Lanita through school with the caveat that Gene live there rent free as long as he wanted. That was her bequeathal to him. The old house she left for me, knowing I would share with Buck. She knew I would care for my brothers and sisters, but she asked me to especially look after Buck.

Three months after she told us of her diagnosis she transitioned from this life to her mansion in God's house. No more pain; but promises of eternal life. No sickness. No fear. No regrets.

We held her funeral at Mount Olive Missionary Baptist, the family church, amid seventy sprays replete with carnations, lilies, and roses. It smelled of warm earth and joy. Heaven await her youthful vigor returned to the womb of the morning. Daddy on her right. I will take my due place to her left one day. From the rising sun to its resting place beyond the horizon, I will praise the name of the Lord for all He has given to me.

Golden Life

RED CADILLAC. BLUE NAVIGATOR. White bicycle. Kept detailed and waxed pearl smooth. Don't matter though. I haven't driven a car since 1999. But I still drove a golf cart with pride and looked for balls in the rough.

Sports injuries derailed my professional sports career. Broken ankle in the eleventh; pin in the left knee in 1955; front tooth in 1956, called time out, rinsed my mouth and finished the game with a win. I graduated toothless. Begged Mama and Daddy for an open-face crown when I graduated. The gold turned my good tooth black. I wish Dr. Smith had warned me, but he was too busy giving money to kids for college. Prophetic.

When I began losing my eyesight, I was reading the bible one night and thought my glasses were dirty. I wondered, "What's going on?" Why am I squinting my eyes? My doctor had recently retired. Okay Mama, I thought. You have got to get me in to see the doctor. Mama took care of my doctor's appointments; but she forgot about the ophthalmologist. Glaucoma. Advancing, like me, in age, but not mind and body. That was twenty years ago, when I still had time to do the things I wanted to do, when grass hadn't yet grown under foot, and keys hung closely by the door.

I got scheduled for surgery as soon as possible. Twenty years later, I am totally blind in my left eye. No split, no depth perception, no peripheral vision of interest. Looks like I'm peeking through a peephole and darkness is looking back at me. To know you, stand directly in front of me, jump up and down two times, and sing "Rough side of the Mountain."

Had I only myself to rely on relying on others wouldn't be so bad. But now I wait on my couch for a ride, and my patience gets tested again. Can't ride my bicycle to work. I retired in 1997 because I couldn't see out of my right eye. I've always been independent. I don't like to be late, but I have to wait for everyone to take me from point A to point B because the doctors said by 1998, I might be blind.

I need someone to take me to church on Sunday, so I stay lifted in prayer. I don't like waiting for anyone. But still, I wait on the Lord. We were in church sharing testimonials and Mama said, "He's not going blind. God got too much for him to do." On another occasion, when the same topic of conversation arose, Delores said, "If he does lose his sight, then I'll be his eyes."

And still, I prefer to do things myself. That way I know it gets done and feelings stay where they belong—at the mouth of Okeechobee, flowing uninterrupted. No one gets hurt. Too much hurt already. Knees creak late in the night and when the barometric pressure drops low.

I have always made lemonade when life has served me lemons. Mama taught me all things are redeemable; including kissing too many girls and pride. I tried to protect myself from becoming trapped by a woman. So, for a long time I didn't want to marry anyone until I was ready to be married.

Delores and I dated fourteen years before we said I do. We traveled and went to events together, shared thoughts and ideas, confidences, and ambitions. To be frank with you, I don't think any other women could have completed my life like Delores has. She never pressured me to marry her. If ever I was given an ultimatum by any woman I dated, the door closed. Pushing me in a corner doesn't make me yield.

It was four or five months before I brought Delores to meet Mama. After a few get-togethers, she said, "You got a winner. I hope you don't blow this one." The family loved her; Daddy, Faye, and my boys. She was easy to fall in love with. Plus, I don't know a more beautiful Black woman.

During our courtship, her mother was diagnosed with stage four cancer and asked to see me. I drove to Hope Sound where she said, "Danny, I need you to promise me two things. I want you to help Delores get my three sons to me before I die." They were scattered across the country and didn't get home often. Then, laying there on her sick bed she took my hand and said, "Promise me you will always look after Delores." She didn't ask me to marry her, just to look after her. I assured her I would. She couldn't know her daughter would one day look after me.

I was running "the Unsung Hero," an annual award gala that recognizes and celebrates accomplishments of individuals doing things in the community. It was one of the Associations fundraising events too. We had a tough time each year raising enough money to keep the program going so playfully announced I was laying down the hat and retiring.

"Since we are having trouble raising enough money to keep the organization afloat, I'm going to retire, relocate to Phoenix, Arizona, and marry Delores."

I was trying to get a rise out of the three hundred fifty people since I had already threatened that I was to retire. Delores and Mama hugged. "This is the best thing that could have ever happened," Mama said. "I thought I'd be dead and buried before you two married."

Delores began planning the wedding. It dragged on for a few months before Mama asked, "Delores, am I going to see you get married before the old lady leaves this earth?" Delores told Mama, "That's up to your son, Mrs. Calloway."

"Mama," I yelled. "Leave it alone."

We talked about having the wedding at Mt. Olive, but it was too small. Our list grew to the point of overwhelm. My dilemma was who to ask to be my best man. Everyone suggested that I take the straightforward way out and ask Buck, since he was closest to me. But then I'd leave Junior out. And what about my friends? It became too much so I told Delores I wanted to do something different. We didn't tell anyone our plans until we arrived in California and I called Mama. I kept it from everyone. Didn't tell Buck or Gene, and none of my friends. On June 25, 1995 Delores and I were married in Hawaii. End of the year we had a praise-worthy reception at the Colonnade.

I have tried to never take Delores for granted. We both keep busy schedules, making it hard for us to travel and do the things we once did together. And honestly, I've gotten older and more comfortable slowing down. But she has never put anything ahead of my well-being when she goes out of town. She calls everyone to let them know when she is leaving and returning, making sure I am cared for in her absence. I am reminded of a story that you might have already heard me share.

We go to Sunday service every week at the family church. During Sunday service, the preacher said bring all you have and put it on the table. Two wealthy men put one hundred dollars in the collection basket. The old lady gave a widow mite and ten pence, and it was all she had. Jesus said she had given more than every other because she gave all she had. The little boy went home and asked for a nickel. He went by the table. Instead of passing by and not doing anything, he jumped into the basket.

The minister asked him, "Son, what are you are doing?"

"Well, Reverend. Last week you said we must give all we have. I don't have a nickel. I only have myself so I'm giving you all of me." Delores, thank you for giving me all you have.

Just imagine, a shoulder injury opened up for me a whole new world; a life unimagined beyond the stars. I just had to remain open to be a servant instead of the served. In the process, I was put to the test. God opened the windows of heaven, poured down for me His blessings, and used my talents to fulfil His purpose for my life. His hand remains upon me still.